How to japan

A Tokyo Correspondent's Take

Colin Joyce

How to Japan
A Tokyo Correspondent's Take

Copyright © 2009 by Colin Joyce
ISBN 978-4-14-035084-3 C0082
All rights reserved. Published in Japan by NHK Publishing, Inc. (NHK Shuppan)

No part of this book may be used or reproduced in any manner whatsoever
without written permission, except in the case of brief quotations
embodied in critical articles and reviews.

For information:
NHK Publishing, Inc. (NHK Shuppan)
41-1 Udagawacho, Shibuya, Tokyo, 150-8081, Japan
http://www.nhk-book.co.jp

Printed in Japan

Book Design by Takeshi Hatanaka

Foreword to the English Edition

This book had an unusual genesis. Shiro Hayashi of NHK Publishing read some of my columns about life in Tokyo in *Newsweek Japan* magazine and was struck with an idea: Would I be interested in writing a book as if I was explaining about Japan for a Western readership? The twist was that all along we knew it would be published in Japanese and would, therefore, have an almost exclusively Japanese readership.

This approach seems to have confused some people, because when the book came out we had several enquiries from readers about where to find the English "original". Well, more than two years later, here it is.

If I were really writing to explain Japan to another English person, I would have written a rather different book. For one thing, I assume a certain level of knowledge about—and interest in—Japan. And there are also parts where I am clearly speaking to a Japanese readership.

The Japanese version of this book was published in December 2006. Some things have changed since then. Most notably, I have left Japan and am no longer the Tokyo correspondent for *The Daily Telegraph*. We decided, however, to publish this in the original form as my "take" on things at that time, when I was in my fifteenth year in Japan and struggling to do my best as an English reporter in Tokyo.

In one sense, it took a long time to produce this book. It came out almost exactly ten years after my first article about Japan was published. In another sense, it was done at breakneck speed. I remember writing several chapters in the space of four days in a hotel room in Yokohama—and the final edit being done in a matter of days.

I think the book reflects both those factors. I feel it provides a good overview of how I felt about the country I had lived in for so long. And there are places I wish I could have expressed myself better, or more economically, or had researched a bit deeper before writing.

Many people helped me with this book. In particular, Mr Hayashi, Shizuka Takamori and Takeshi Nakano of NHK Publishing. Takehiko Tanioka's polished translation was crucial to the success of the Japanese version. Todd Neff helped me find numerous errors in the English script. *Newsweek Japan* gave me

Foreword to the English Edition

my first job in journalism and colleagues there supported me as I developed. Many friends patiently listened to me expound my views on life in Japan, correcting my misunderstandings and allowing me to hone my favourite stories. My family in England helped me by always keeping a home for me. The faults that remain are mine entirely.

July 2009

CONTENTS

Foreword to the English Edition 3

Preface 9

(1) **The Reflecting Pool** 14

(2) **"Japanese is Easy"** 20

(3) **The Joys of Japanese** 28

(4) **First Impressions; 'evanescent, strange and charming'** 36

(5) **Tokyo Vistas** 45

(6) **Mr. Manners and Me** 50

(7) **"Made in Japan" Inventions** 55

(8) **The Not-Lost Decade** 63

- **9**   **Turning Japanese** 72
- **9.5**   **Every Day is April Fool's** 80
- **10**   **Loving an Unlovely City** 85
- **11**   **Let's Tokyo** 97
- **12**   **Two Island Nations** 107
- **13**   **Temperate Island Gifts** 117
- **14**   **Confessions of a Tokyo Correspondent** 125
- **15**   **Gaijin Dilemmas** 139
- **16**   **Smells Like Pickled Eel** 147
- **17**   **Letter to an Incoming Correspondent** 159

Preface

"Tokyo? Really? What's it like?"

I have lost count of the number of times I have been asked that.

But it always sparks off three questions of my own: Do you really want to know or do you want me to condense a world of information into one line? Where do I start? And how do I explain?

There have been times when I delivered the one-liners to people I knew weren't really interested: "Very Japanese" was my favourite answer for a while (and most succinct).

Other times I mocked the British obsession with weirdy Japan stories: "Man, you should see how big Konishiki's bum is."

Or I played on their ignorance and gullibility: "It's like the future has already arrived. The rice store in my neighbourhood used to be run by an old lady but they just replaced her with a robot." (You'd be amazed. Sometimes people will believe that line.)

Other times, I played the expat and bemoaned the difficulties of adapting to life overseas: "Unbelievably crowded, hot in summer, lots of earthquakes, not many parks and a pint costs five pounds."

But then there are people who really want to know. They are interested in Japan — but not in the way they are interested in, say, football. They don't have a wealth of knowledge that they wish to deepen. At best, they will know *The Magnificent Seven* was inspired by Kurosawa's *Seven Samurai*. Few will be able to argue whether Ozu or Kurosawa was the greater.

Most will have a few disparate bits of information from which they can form no complete picture: healthy 100-year-olds — *"genki rojin"*—skiing down mountains, *kaitenzushi*, boring politicians, clever robots...

In other words, they really don't get it.

It can be easy for me to forget after twelve years in Tokyo but, for many Westerners, Japan is the most exotic place on earth. (I have heard that exact expression from a Japanophile Brit). I have heard Japan called "unknowable" by an Australian writer, as though it is a country that defies understanding. I disagree. It just takes longer to get to know and the answers are often not what you expect.

There is a cultural gap that can be hard to cross. A Brit visiting Germany has less of a leap. There is the

Preface

problem of a language that seems indecipherable. (I remember when I first came to Japan that the words sounded "slippery". I couldn't hang on to them in my head long enough and couldn't catch where one word ended and another started.) The way people behave is different, for better or worse. An outsider struggles to know how far he should adapt and how much he needs to retain his own original settings.

It can all be so bamboozling that a visitor can become terrified that he is committing dreadful social faux pas all the time. I think of Micheal Palin, the *Monty Python* star, who visited Japan for a BBC travel programme. After being told he should remove his slippers when he entered a *tatami* room, he became nervous about how to eat, convinced that there must be a strict order for which plate to eat from first.

Certain things just don't make sense. Writing stories for British newspapers, I am often put on the spot by my editors. "How can an ex-prime minister be powerful?" or, "What is a faction?" they ask. Other times, assuming editorial comments must be the same the world over, they ask me to insert a powerful quote of condemnation or praise from the *Yomiuri*. They don't believe me when I tell them the paper's view is "on the one hand . . . on the other hand . . . " then, in conclusion, "serious consideration is needed on this matter".

Perhaps it's these differences and idiosyncrasies that make people ask about Japan. The curiosity manifests itself in ongoing enthusiasm for Japan's exotic cultures such as sumo and geisha. But also people love to read about robot fish and dancing robots. (What are they for?) I have written about Takarazuka Revue (women playing men and other women playing extremely girly women!), about *otaku*, about drunken *hanami* parties, about the millions of lost property items dutifully handed in each year in Tokyo . . . Perhaps Japanese won't be pleased to hear this but their country fascinates with its odd crimes: from harems in Western Tokyo and the emergence of "grey crime" (crimes committed by the elderly) to cults and gangsters.

Amid all these stories, it is easy to get a slanted view of Japan. I am embarrassed to admit that at the *Telegraph* I probably write more whacky stories than politics stories. Believe me, we cover the elections and constitutional debate. Sometimes we even do big, prominent pieces. But when I ask my friends back home, the story they remember is the super-function toilet, not the Koizumi analysis.

Preface

It can be hard to write for a readership that little understands Japan. It seems people can only hold one image at a time. You can write stories that illustrate a stereotype (*karoshi* "death from overwork") or write stories that defy the stereotype (young people drop out of Japan Inc. and pursue hobbies as "*freeters*"). But subtler stories in between somehow don't work.

Once, in the space of a week I proposed two stories: one on Japan's sexless marriages and another on shotgun weddings. My editor was confused: Are the Japanese bonking like bunnies or giving up on sex? Which is it?

I bit my lip irritably and resisted snapping back that, in a country of 127 million people, of course there is going to be more than one discernible trend.

Instead, I tried to look at it positively. He did ask. He wanted to know. I could hear echoes of the same questions I heard a thousand times: Tokyo? Really? What's it like?

Okay, I'll try to explain . . .

1
The Reflecting Pool

If you want to understand Japanese society, take a trip to a swimming pool. It won't teach you all the intricacies of Japanese life but as a thirty-minute primer you can't beat it. Perhaps it's because there are an awful lot of people crammed into a pretty limited space, rather like Japan. Whenever I take a dip in Tokyo I find myself thinking how the pool is a microcosm of the country as a whole.

The first thing that strikes you is how very ordered it all is. There are clearly defined areas for swimming, mucking about and water walking. It is a monument to the Japanese love of order and safety.

Often, even the swimming lanes are graded, so that beginners and experienced swimmers are separated. But even where the lanes are open to all, people usually manage to self-regulate so that they find the right lane. The view from above reveals a mass of people swimming in neat lines at almost the maximum possible distance from each other. When the inevitable occasional bump occurs it is resolved with a mutual nod of apology. A vision of peace.

1 The Reflecting Pool

Maybe I am going too far here, but it seems even the people in pools tend to conform to the roles expected of them in society. The kids play vigorously, just like they do outside the pool. The old people are amazingly healthy and cheerful, walking and talking. Working people swim. (And if you happen to spot a high school swimming club, they are sure to be training hard—to an alarming degree).

This is all very different from the UK, where a bird's eye view of a pool reveals a scene of indecipherable chaos. Kids are jumping all over the place and screaming. They are supposed to stay out of the deep end, but venture in by pulling themselves along the side of the pool. Anyone attempting to swim is veering wildly from side to side in an effort to get past the next group of teenagers who are standing in groups and tipping each other over. There most likely isn't anyone over 50. If you bump into someone, you probably glare at him glaring back at you.

At a guess I would say that if a Japanese pool continues to function with 100 people, a pool of the same size in England would become unswimmable with 60 people and riots would break out with 80 people. If you have ever seen a Westerner getting obviously stressed at a swimming pool in Japan, it is probably because he finds his tolerance for coping in confined space is breaking down. (That "he" may actually be me.)

English pools do have rules, of course. It's just that no one really bothers to observe them or enforce them. Japan, on the other hand, seems to thrive on a profusion of rules. My favourite example is the five-minute rest rule, whereby even if you have only just gotten into the pool you must get out and take a break at the prescribed time. I cannot resist the temptation to wind up the pool assistants by telling them that I am not at all tired and, indeed, am just getting into my stride.

Then there is the swimming cap rule. No person will be allowed in a pool at any time without a swim cap. I knew an Englishman who always shaved his hair off to conceal the fact that he was balding. They still wouldn't let him in without a cap.

In my first month in Japan, I attended a lecture by the British academic Joy Hendry who explained how one society will often try to castigate another as "dirty", especially if that society is seen as a threat. Unable to pin this charge on the Japanese, a wartime American study did the next best thing and labeled the Japanese "pathologically clean". Thus they managed to make an

1 THE REFLECTING POOL

insult out of a compliment.

Sometimes I think I know what they meant though. There is a pool in Beppu with the stated aim of being the "cleanest pool in all Japan". I can't imagine such a sign in another country. Perhaps in Britain the sign might read: "We aim to reach a passable standard of cleanliness and then not worry about it too much."

So, rules make Japanese pools work. But for the newcomer it can all seem a bit much. "The *urusai* pool" was what one little boy from Rome called the Tokyo pool he visited with his Japanese mum. Not *urusai* to mean "noisy", but rather "too much ordering you around".

I myself once had a brush with Japanese pool authorities. Impatiently waiting during a compulsory break, I got back in the pool seconds before the whistle went, and pushed off while the lifeguard was still reading some announcements.

When I surfaced I was scolded for premature entry ("yes, I know"), swimming underwater ("but only a few strokes, surely that's okay"), not wearing my cap ("oh, I must have taken it off during the break") and SWIMMING UP THE DOWN LANE ("whoops"). Four rule breaches in one go! And none of them would have raised an eyebrow in England.

A pool also reflects the incredible patience of the Japanese. For example, when a very slow swimmer gets into a "medium" swimming lane. Sometimes a whole line of swimmers switch to breaststroke and form a patient queue behind the dawdler, hoping in vain for the problem to disappear. Other times, people begin to switch lanes one after another, so that six or seven people will inconvenience themselves rather than politely suggesting to one person that he might prefer a slower lane. Since overtaking is forbidden (another rule), people sometimes take to flipping around and swimming back the other way when they approach the obstructing slowcoach. Then they have to do this again in a couple of lengths' time.

Perhaps this deference to the individual is a virtue—even if it does inconvenience a lot of people. Perhaps that patience is what makes an overcrowded archipelago livable.

But I also have to say that Japan shows inordinate respect to big groups. I think of how 20-strong groups at *izakaya* yell and shout, without anyone regard for the couple at the next table trying to have a chat. At one outdoor pool in Meguro where I often swim in the summer, there is a phenomenon that occurs daily at around 7:15 in the evening. A group of fifteen or

1 THE REFLECTING POOL

more regular swimmers get together and swim quickly up and down in a line. They splash a lot, make a fair bit of noise and are apparently oblivious to the fact that this is annoying to individual swimmers. They are pool *bōsōzoku*. I have to say it's a weakness of Japan that it lets large groups get away with behaving badly. From my mostly harmless fellow swimmers at Meguro to real *bōsōzoku* to yakuza, it's as if by being a big group you get to decide your own rules.

But now I really am reading too much into all this. The pool is nice and clean. It only cost a few hundred yen. It's all very well-ordered. The young lifeguards are typically earnest, not just slouching around and chatting. Perhaps I should just enjoy the swim. It's a nice country . . . I mean pool.

2
"Japanese is Easy"

"Japanese is easy." I always wanted to say that just once. When I finally did, the reaction was as if I had said "the earth is flat" or "The Beatles are over-rated".

The reputation of Japanese is that it is devilishly hard to learn. It's a view held not only by Westerners but by the Japanese themselves. To some extent, I can see why—all that squiggly writing. But that can't explain it in full.

In Britain, so few people learn Japanese that hardly anyone knows first-hand what it's like—or even second-hand from a friend. Meanwhile, the Japanese can't really judge if their language is hard as they never really learned it, just picked it up as they went along. (In the same way, I have a limited understanding of what's easy and what's difficult about English).

I think the fiendish reputation of Japanese is based largely on a shared perception that we are very different. I don't even mean this in a bad way. In a shrinking world, I think there is an unconscious thirst for some rare land where people don't all drink coffee at Starbucks and watch *Friends*.

2 "Japanese is Easy"

To some extent Japan fills that need. Few British people have been to Japan—a lot fewer than Thailand, for example. And Japan has some exotic and powerful traditions that exist nowhere else. What could complete the picture more perfectly than a language so subtle and complex that we cannot begin to grasp it?

Then there's the problem of those of us who have learned Japanese. The fact is that we have a vested interest in continuing the myth of a dastardly difficult language. It makes people think we are not just clever, but somewhat more mysterious and "other". And there's little chance anyone is going to contradict us.

"You speak Japanese? I hear it's the most difficult language..." people ask me. As a journalist I suppose I have a duty at least to try to get the truth across.

I first said "Japanese is easy" to get someone's attention, but in fact you can make quite a strong case that it is.

Pronunciation is straightforward thanks to the limited range of sounds. (The words I had to practice most were *udon* and *ryokan*. The ones I still mess up most regularly are *sakka*—writer—and *sakkā*—football). Intonation is easy; just start by keeping it as flat as you can.

There is no number or gender or case for nouns.

There is no indefinite or definite article.

Tenses are simple. I genuinely can't remember if there are any irregular verbs—if there are, I sweated no blood to learn them.

Nor are adjectives particularly troublesome. There are only two types of adjective, and it is almost always possible to recognize which type by the word's ending.

Usually, all of those kinds of things render learning foreign languages a perfect pain. How ingenious of Japanese to have evolved a language that does away with these problems. I hope no specialist reads this, but I think the logical nature of Japanese makes it much easier for children to learn it than English. I have heard Japanese children make occasional errors, such as saying "*kireikatta*" instead of "*kirei datta*". But little English boys are full of grammatical hilarities: "I eated it", "nice peoples" and "Canadans".

"Ah, but," some people retort, "Japanese has *keigo* and female speech. You have to learn two whole new ways of speaking to master Japanese." It seems to me that Japanese struggle about as much as foreign students do with *keigo* (formal language). It must be a shock, after 18 years of speaking your native tongue, to be expected to speak it differently. But for me it

2 "Japanese is Easy"

consisted largely of learning about eight extra verbs. Then you throw in a bit more bowing than usual and you're pretty much there. As for women's speech, does anyone use it except voice actresses dubbing foreign films?

True, counting in Japanese can be complex. *Ippon, nihiki, sanwa, yontō, itsutsu* etc. But, as a survival strategy, a learner can get around this by sticking to *hitotsu, futatsu*. Anyway, it's hard to worry about getting it wrong when plenty of Japanese don't know that two pairs of chopsticks are *nizen* or that three rabbits are *sanwa*. Personally I rather enjoyed this little complication because of its humour potential. It's great fun to say with a straight face that your sister is expecting her second child (*nihikime*). Or you can quiz Japanese people earnestly on whether two *kappa* are *nihiki, nitō* or *niwa*? And what is the correct counter for a blob of jam?

But then I have to admit there is some stuff about Japanese that make it hard to learn—or at least different from learning other languages.

For one thing, the people you are talking to are compulsive flatterers. "*Nihongo ojōzu desune. Pera pera desuyo*," they say. I remember the first time I was told this because I had no idea what I was being told.

Later a friend explained that *ojōzu* was just the same as *jōzu* (good at). And that *pera pera* means fluent. I laughed at the irony of not being able to understand someone telling me I was a master of Japanese.

Speaking ten or twelve words of English will not bring in garlands of praise in Britain. Indeed, you will likely be the object of intense frustration: "What on earth are you trying to say man?"

Perhaps we students of Japanese should be grateful for the encouragement. But at a certain point it becomes absurd. I remember thinking: "Please stop telling me I am a genius. I haven't learned the word for 'clothes' yet."

On the other hand, there is the surprisingly regular occurrence of not being able to convince people that you are speaking their language. You always know this is happening when the person you are talking to either looks at you too intensely, starts waving his hand across his face or yelps out an "eh?" before you have finished your sentence. All sorts of self-doubt can kick in.

One day I realized that I had not only to speak Japanese better, I had to speak it *differently* from Japanese.

While my teacher told us "*Tanaka desu*" is a

2 "Japanese is Easy"

perfectly good way to introduce oneself, I noticed that "*Colin desu*" isn't. "*Watashi wa Colin to iimasu*," cleared everything up.

I also noticed that saying "*sumimasenga* . . . " and waiting three seconds before proceeding was very helpful. This, it seems, is the time it takes many Japanese to realize that the white person in front of them is speaking Japanese.

It's lucky that Japanese is quite easy to pronounce because you need to be quite accurate. In London, we are used to hearing all sorts of people murder our language. Having your native tongue spoken badly is perhaps the cost of having it as the global language. Indeed, in a world with more non-native speakers of English than native speakers, perhaps we can no longer even talk about an absolute standard of correct pronunciation.

All this is quite different from Japan, where the vast majority of people are only used to hearing other native speakers of Japanese. To deviate from this by even a small margin is therefore to invoke incomprehension.

One of the great oddities of Japanese is that learners can speak before they read. When people learn French or German, they start picking up words and sentences from newspapers fairly soon. Conversation comes later. In Japanese, being able to read a newspaper is considered a mighty challenge—one that separates the wheat from the chaff.

The story of the Japanese writing system is a classic historical mishap. It would be funny were it not for the intense years of study it forces on us all (Japanese people too). The Japanese learned to write from China: a country with a writing system not only bizarrely complex but also totally structurally unsuited to Japanese.

If only Japan had waited patiently for a few centuries until a better choice presented itself. (Of course, my recommendation would be the alphabet.) Or Japan could have thought up its own system. But no, *kanji* it was—and that required the invention of *kana* to make the words make sense. Then *katakana* was warped into a system for loan words. Then the Japanese decided that dropping a smattering of *romaji* words into text would do no harm.

I tell this to friends in England and they shake their heads in disbelief. Japanese writing is a formidable inconvenience.

It reminds me of two other favourite historical cock-ups. Apparently, way back in the early days of the automobile, cars ran on steam or petrol. Just at that time, there was a drought in the US while oil seemed to exist in limitless abundance. The industry opted for petrol and a hundred years of ingenuity went into making better and better internal combustion engines. There were plenty of advantages to steam-based external combustion engines, but today it is rather late to start again.

The other is the qwerty line-up of the keyboard. It was devised that way to keep common combinations of letters apart, so that as people bashed away on typewriters the metal rods would shoot up from various angles without clashing. Of course, all it ensures today is that computer keyboards have the most common letters spread all over the place.

Okay, okay. Japanese isn't exactly easy. It's hard to get started and it's hard to finish the job. But it's logical enough to let you make steady progress. Besides, the native speakers are quite patient—and the rewards make up for the struggles.

3
The Joys of Japanese

When I started learning Japanese I used to have a recurring, nightmarish, thought. One day, thanks to computers and superior understanding of the brain, it will be possible to programme people to speak and understand a foreign language. It would be poured into them in their sleep somehow. Or perhaps it would just become totally unnecessary—in the near future we would need only to slip our interpreting devices into our ears for us all to be able to communicate freely, speaking our own languages.

I would look at the page of *kanji* I was trying—and failing—to remember, then look at the hundreds and hundreds to go and feel resentment about the complete waste of time it was all going to be. Deep inside, a well of jealousy formed towards those lucky people—five or ten years from now—who would laugh at all the effort I put into learning Japanese in the days before "the great breakthrough".

What I wish someone had told me then was not just that my fantasy was bizarre (or at least a generation away) but that learning a language is

3 THE JOYS OF JAPANESE

worthwhile in itself. Specifically with Japanese there is the ego-pleasing factor of conquering a language few of your countrymen speak and most think is "impossible". But even greater is the sheer delight of finding something so clever or insightful or just plain funny that it knocks me sideways.

To start with, Japanese has some superb expressions. "Even a monkey falls from a tree" is perhaps the first that any student of Japanese learns. It may also be the best. "*Saru mo ki kara ochiru*" combines a series of simple words familiar to a beginner, while collectively expressing the concept of fallibility so much more powerfully and amusingly than the English "nobody's perfect".

I wonder if any Japanese get the same pleasure as I from "*neko ni koban*"? Its English equivalent is "pearls before swine" but I somehow love the idea of "giving coins to a cat". I think of my own boyhood cat, Gimmerley, and the look of total indifference she could summon up on occasions. "*Neko ni koban*" is a triumph of economy—just three words—and a masterpiece of imagery.

More recently I heard a slang expression (not featured in any dictionary) that was of such complex and remarkable ingenuity that I hoped to write a story on it. A British journalist friend beat me to it. "*Zenbei ga naita*" ("All of America wept") is apparently used sarcastically to express contempt for a product or service. The convoluted logic is that since the hackneyed expression is used in Japanese advertisements for so many substandard films emanating from the US, that it can be applied to anything that is disappointing, over-rated or just crap. The originality of this usage blows away two of the common misapprehensions about Japanese: that they are short on humour and that they are suckers for all things American.

Sometimes it is the sheer illogic of Japanese that amazes me. How can "*me ga nai*" (to "not have eyes") mean "to like" something? Surely it means you can't stand even to look at it?

Many years ago a kindly Japanese colleague invited me to his house for dinner, or so I thought until he dropped me off at the station. Noticing my bewilderment he repeated "*kondo, kondo*". "This time," I translated in my head. So why is he driving off? Later a friend explained *kondo* means "next time". If that is the case, then surely *konshū* means "next week".

Yappari is also a favourite word. It can mean "yes" or "no", "however", "as I expected", or, indeed,

3 THE JOYS OF JAPANESE

absolutely nothing at all. Every language should have such a word. Politicians would love it as it frees them from having to express an opinion. And of course it has inbuilt deniability. You can always claim your *yappari* meant the exact opposite of what people thought you said.

Japan is also rich in words of a single syllable. Some even have only one letter when put into *romaji*. *U* (cormorant) is my favourite—and incidentally one of my first words in Japanese. How I delighted in telling friends that you could theoretically say "a picture of a cormorant's stomach and tail" (35 letters in English) in just ten letters in Japanese: "*u no i to o no e.*"

Then there are the words that just sound funny. Or perhaps they only sound funny to me? To Japanese they are words that mean something, whereas to me they are initially just sounds. "*Zunguri mukkuri*" has to be the among the most comical arrangement of sounds in any language.

Japanese also has the most fascinating and comprehensive collection of onomatopoeia and phenomimes (or *giseigo* and *gitaigo* as I always call them). There is an entire book devoted to them for students, while numerous websites explore this rich area of Japanese. Some of them, we Japanese learners acquire almost immediately—*pera pera,* which Japanese use flatteringly when we stutter out a few words, or *ira ira,* which describes my agitated state when I'm trying to squeeze through crowded train stations. Recently I tried to count how many of these types of words I knew and came up with 58. Of course there are dozens more and I always listen out for new ones.

Giseigo and *gitaigo* constitute a form of "national treasure", which can add great variety, clarity and humour to conversation when used appropriately. *Shiku shiku* (the sound of someone crying) may be the one I like best. A friend uses *pachi pachi* (the sound of applause) to great effect. But I would ask Japanese people to please remember that a foreigner is not going to guess what these "sound words" mean until they have learned them. A student will understand "*onaka suiteiru?*" (the standard expression for "are you hungry?") before "*onaka peko peko?*" I still don't think *peko peko* summons images of emptiness. That hungover morning ten years ago I could have answered "*atama itai?*" ("does your head hurt?") but not "*atama gan gan tte kanji?*" Though I do see how *gan gan* implies throbbing.

Another great Japanese invention is the random

3 The Joys of Japanese

and unpredictable way it picks up and incorporates English. *Pasokon*, of course, is incomprehensible to an English speaker—but altogether more user-friendly than PC. *Mazakon*, of course, isn't even derived from English. We say Oedipus complex, which is actually less straightforward than the Japanese because it requires a certain knowledge of ancient Greek drama.

At *Newsweek Japan* magazine I always wondered what the editor meant when he announced "*stokkon*". Nine years after I first heard it, a friend explained it was "story conference". Similarly, colleagues dropped the words "better" and "plus alpha" into discussions in Japanese. The former, I reasoned, couldn't be the English word "better" because Japanese already has a word for that (and surely that is better). "Plus alpha" I had never heard before in English. I hear some offices use "NR" for "not return" —an expression that, if ever used in England, might imply someone had died.

"Must item" drops the word "have" from the middle perhaps because it fits poorly into *katakana*? But judging from words like *choberiba* (from the Japanese "*chō*" for "extreme" and from the English "very bad"), Japanese doesn't seem to care about messing with the original words. Mixing up Japanese and English like this demonstrates a certain talent for adopting and localising foreign terms. The *okushon* (from "1 *oku mansion*", to mean "100 million yen apartment") is a great example of this—playful and informative at the same time. This leads me to the Japanese trick of completely changing the meaning of a word. In English a "mansion" is not "a tiny apartment without room to swing a cat". The word "Viking" makes me think of a marauding tribe of Scandinavian pirates, not a buffet.

After many years learning Japanese I can perhaps rank my three favourite expressions as follows. At number three is *"shōbu pants"*. I have never explained "victory pants" to a friend who hasn't loved it. What other language could be so honest as to have a term for the underwear you put on for an important date? *Bridget Jones' Diary* was so popular because it came out and said many of the things that millions of single women had previously thought that only they thought. That includes her knicker-changing at crucial moments. Secretly, millions of women (and not a few men) thought: "Others do it too!" If they had only known Japanese, they would have realized it is common practise.

At number two is *"uwame-zukai"*. I hadn't been in Japan for long when I noticed that some women have

3 The Joys of Japanese

a trick of staring up through forlorn or pleading eyes, like a child, in an attempt to gain some kind of favour. It was many years of jokingly imitating it before someone told me Japanese has a word for it. And it is simply "using up-eyes". Genius.

But my all-time favourite word is "*o-nyū*". The first time I heard it I laughed aloud and spend much of the day thinking about it. The mix of the English word "new" with a Japanese honorific; the way it captures that temporary feeling of pleasure you get from something you use for the first time; the humour and irony. To think that you could achieve all that with the addition of a single letter to a short word.

I was glad there was no device in my ear that just translated it into English for me.

4
First Impressions;
'evanescent, strange and charming'

Stupid, stupid, stupid. I should have at least made some notes.

A kindly teacher had told me to write down my first impressions of Japan, in fact quoting how a kindly professor had told exactly that to Lafcadio Hearn.

My only excuse is that the great Lafcadio also failed to do so.

And yet, much seems engraved on my memory from my first few months in Japan many years ago as one of a group of British students in Kobe. Perhaps because I viewed it as a big adventure, not just a year at a new school. I was acutely aware that it was my first time outside Europe. I had never learned any foreign language beyond the very basics, and even those I had long forgotten.

I remember on the plane experiencing my first Japanese meal. Or at least I remember swallowing a horrible fiery little bright green lump of food and thinking: "If this is Japanese cuisine I'm not going to like it." I did, however, like that my soy sauce came in a little transparent plastic fish. I kept it as a souvenir.

4 First Impressions: 'evanescent, strange and charming'

When we land the air feels damp, which is new to me. A friend intones: "It's not heat that kills you, it's the humidity."

A Japanese student from the school has come to meet us at the airport. He repeats his name for me twice. "Kidell," I heard. He looks about 18. Later, we establish he is "Hideo" and he is nearly 30.

The school where I am to study, and its adjacent dormitory, is high above Kobe. The night view over the bay blows me away. England has few mountains and my home county of Essex is among the flattest places on earth. I awake early and watch in wonder at how the scenery changes with the growing light.

But I am bothered by the awful noise the "electricity generators" are making. A few days later a Japanese friend explains that the noise is cicadas. In that instant the sound is transformed to something altogether more pleasant.

Below my room on my very first night I can just make out the shape of people in a park. The park is oval with a path around it. In the dark, I conclude it is a running track and that the figure I see is a *"samurai* salaryman" remorselessly forcing himself to run a few laps after a long day at the office.

Over the next few days I find the park at night is

almost exclusively peopled by couples there for the night view. I remind myself not to think in stereotypes.

Days later, on my first Friday night in town, I witness drunken, red-faced salarymen staggering about. The sight shatters any lingering illusions of "straight-laced" Japanese men.

A urinal flushes as I walk up to it and again as I leave. I instinctively giggle. Sensors on toilets! I am to learn that in Japan there are super-advanced toilets. And incredibly primitive ones.

The shapes of many things are subtly but disturbingly wrong. The bath is too short and weirdly deep. The loaves of bread are hilariously short, but the slices disconcertingly thick. The baths I come to love. The "six-slice loaves" I come to accept—if only because bread goes mouldy so quickly in the humid months that it's best to buy in small quantities.

Japanese milk, by contrast, lasts for weeks. In England it goes off within a day or two in summer.

We head into town of an evening. At Sannomiya, I am at first excited by all the neon lights. I soon learn they are just a mirage, promising much but in fact only testament to the bad taste and deep pockets of the companies paying for them.

I am taken to a karaoke box with friends. I find it

4 First Impressions; 'evanescent, strange and charming'

sterile and uninteresting to lock ourselves in a room away from the world outside. I am so disappointed that I make my way back on the bus alone. Surrounded by Japanese people, I feel a mixture of tension and excitement. It strikes me that I am, perhaps for the first time, something exotic.

Walking through Osaka, I see something unusual and point it out to my Japanese teacher. He cannot guess what I am looking at because it is totally normal to him. It is the contraption that holds delivery meals in place on the back of motorbikes. (Years later, something similar happens in reverse. An English friend remarks "how clever" something is. It takes me a while to establish that she means my "Made in Japan" bicycle lock, which coils up when not in use and slots neatly into a holder beneath the seat.)

I find Japanese children unbelievably, unbearably cute. (The year I arrive in Japan unicycles are very popular with kids for some reason.) Japanese people, I am interested to hear, find Western children incredibly cute in just the same way.

I go to see Oxford, my old university, play Kobe Steel at rugby. I get lost on the way. A kindly man takes me to the stadium by taxi and insists on paying. He cannot speak English and all I can say is *"arigato"* ten times. I am late and my friends with the tickets have gone in without me. The stadium officials let me in anyway. We later christen the ability to overcome these little problems "*gaijin* power".

I find myself among the Steelers fans. I am worried in case this causes trouble. After all, I have heard Japanese people are deeply committed to their companies. I resolve not to cheer if Oxford score. When they do, the Japanese clap politely. I am moved by the courtesy and sportsmanship.

I find my friends and am given my first *bentō*. It looks so neat, with all its little compartments, that I get my picture taken with it.

I try hitch-hiking to Hiroshima but totally underestimate the distance. Instead I only make it as far as Himeji, where I am invited to stay the night by the lovely family who picked me up. They ask me what Japanese food I like and I reply "sushi". I had thought it was just a general question and am aghast when I find they have ordered a feast of sushi. Japanese hospitality.

They also have beer. In England it is good manners to finish what is in front of you. Dozens of times I drain my glass and swear each time to myself that this is the last. While I am distracted, someone refills it. I drink way too much in my efforts to be polite. Mind

4 First Impressions: 'evanescent, strange and charming'

the culture gap.

The limits of my Japanese are obvious. I try to tell the son of the house he has two beautiful sisters. "*Ni kirei ane desu*," I say. "Is that correct?" I ask. "Yes," he replies. So I write my new expression in my "Useful Japanese" notebook.

The daughter's husband is a young salaryman who responds to my "*yoroshiku*" with "I am pleased to meet you" in a perfect accent. I assume he speaks fluent English and call repeatedly for his help. Eventually I realize he knows precisely one sentence of English.

I often walk around the *shōtengai* shopping arcade listening to British indie pop on my Walkman. The divergence between what I see and what I hear is odd.

My friend's birthday falls on a sunny day in mid-October. We play football in the park and laugh at the joy of such lovely weather when people will be shivering in England. I love the way people enjoy Sundays in much the same way as Saturdays. Back then, Sundays in England were an interminable bore. Shops shut, trains didn't run, even the television was rubbish. I feel I have gained an extra day each week.

I learn to love Japanese food. But it digests so quickly compared to my usual fare that between meals I am so hungry I cannot study.

"If Japanese food is so healthy, why am I putting on weight?" I wonder. It turns out that not all Japanese food is healthy. *Takoyaki* and *okonomiyaki*, which I consume with great regularity, contain quite a lot of calories for example.

Learning Japanese is a terrible struggle for me and one other student. It saps my confidence a great deal.

I meet a man called Mr Osaki. I have already learned that there is o-sake and Osaka. I will need to be careful with similar-sounding words.

My fellow students and I make mistakes in Japanese. One friend is taking people's names as they arrive for a party. "*Onamae chigaimasu,*" he says instead of "*onamae onegaishimasu*". ("Your name is wrong," rather than "your name please?") Another tries to express delight with his meal by saying "*onaka wa tenjō ni arimasu!*" ("My stomach is on the ceiling.") He is trying to say: "My stomach is in heaven." When offered something we want, several of us improvise by saying "*ii desu*". ("It's good.") There is a lot of confusion until we are told that this is the way to refuse something.

I visit a shrine and a Japanese man is curious if I said a prayer. "Yes, because I think the Japanese gods are kind," I want to say. But somehow *kami-sama* (gods) becomes *o-kama* (homosexuals). How did I make such a blunder? Firstly, I knew there was an honorific involved, but put the prefix *o-* instead of the suffix *-sama*. Then I simply got the word *kami* wrong, just as I kept calling *sake*, "*saki*". The man had no idea how to take to my strange response.

In Japan I feel poorer than I ever have before. I teach English privately to a few people, who are very generous and kind. But the money just seems to leak away. When people ask me how I like Japan, my standard answer is: "*Bukka ga takai desu.*" ("It's expensive.")

No matter how tired I am, every time I go into town I do the thirty minute walk to Oji Koen station instead of the fifteen minute walk to the bus stop. The train fare is eighty yen cheaper. I hitchhike when I want to travel. In summer, a friend's mother gives me a box of *sōmen* noodles and I eat them for lunch almost daily for weeks. In the evenings I look with envy at people eating and drinking their fill in *izakaya*. I learn that not having money is worse when other people seem to have plenty.

I manage to lose the weight I put on. Then some more.

I wander through a game centre. One man is

"riding" a plastic motorbike around a track projected on a screen before him. I take a picture to show my friends back home.

A homeless man has put his bags in front of a public phone. As I pass the phone, I glance at it. He notices this and hurriedly grabs his bags to move them. He runs after me, calling: "You can use the phone." In Japan, even homeless people are attentive and courteous.

A kindly Japanese family takes me to experience pachinko, even giving me a thousand yen to squander. The game begins. Ping, ping, ping. "But what do I do?" I ask. "By turning the handle you control the projection of the balls," I am told. Ping, ping, ping. "But what's the point?" "You can win money." Ping, ping, ping. All my balls are gone. No one had explained that I was supposed to try to get the balls to fall into the hole in the middle. They assumed I would know that.

A British friend who has worked in Tokyo for a year visits me in Kobe. He seems awfully knowledgeable about Japan and flash with money. It is a bit of a pose, but one that I myself am later guilty of sometimes.

When I am tempted to show off this way, I remind myself that it wasn't very long ago I was eating raw *wasabi* and mistaking insects for machines.

5
Tokyo Vistas

"**Aah** Japan." When some people hear those words they envisage a geisha holding her parasol as she trips lightly between teahouses. Or a monk sitting in silent contemplation in a "Zen garden" . . . Alas, this is rubbish. As any Japanese can tell you, these are scenes you practically never see.

Others hear "Japan" and envisage a Bladerunner-like world, where everything is neon-bright and the future is already happening. One American writer back in the early 1990s talked about Japanese achieving "symbiosis" with computers. Some imagine that the Japanese are our "wired" counterparts, living in "alternative realities", dating "virtual *talento*" created in the ether by corporations run by ex-hackers turned programmers. Except, of course, this image is pretty hard to square with what I see strolling down the little *shōtengai* shopping street in Kuramae, where the grocer puts out vegetables on upturned crates and where few of the stores seem to have had a lick of paint in 20 years. If this is the future, it is decidedly retro.

So what does Japan actually look like? What, the moment you see it, makes you realize you are in Tokyo or Osaka? For me, it is a certain set of images that I have got used to seeing and which I never—or almost never—see outside Japan.

A salaryman sleeps opposite me on the Yamanote Line. He jolts awake at a station, realises instantly where he is and seconds later has crossed the platform for the train heading back the other way.

On a crowded commuter train a man has folded the *Asahi* in an ingenious and complex manner that allows him to read the stories without impinging on the space of the people around him. I think of the cliché about Japanese being clever with their hands and reflect that this is the country that invented origami. In 2003, at great cost, the venerable *Times* of London changed from broadsheet format to tabloid. If the British were able to learn that folding trick from the Japanese *The Times* could have saved itself a fortune and not upset many of its readers.

In the toilets at the *izakaya* there is an unusually deep sink with a large plug-hole and even a hose. I am in a student area of town. For several seconds I cannot decide whether a special sink ideal for vomiting is ingenious or disgraceful. I decide it is at least practical.

5 Tokyo Vistas

The neighbourhood park is tiny but it gives a little bit of shade. A row of taxis, idling while their drivers sleep, make it too noisy and smelly to sit there.

An ashtray on the train platform has caught fire, sending vile smoke across the station. Someone tries to douse it with the dregs of a can of drink. It merely makes it burn more slowly.

Walking along a mostly residential street, I see a family shop selling some unusual delicacy. The last time around it was *ama-nattō*. Sweet *nattō*—what an idea! The store has been there for decades and the "mother" spends 20 minutes recommending choices to me and explaining how each product is made.

I put on the TV and there is a scene of a girl putting some food into her mouth. She says: "*Oishii.*" I flick channels and there is a girl sitting in *onsen* water wearing only a towel. She says: "*Kimochi ii.*" I flick again and there is one of the clowns from the J-Pop band SMAP. (I give up and go back to reading my book.)

It is compulsory break-time at the pool. A man stands in front of me holding one leg behind his back and hops on the other foot with his head leaning sideways. (Apparently this strange Japanese dance dislodges water trapped in your ear.)

Amid the crowds at Hachiko, a girl with her ear pressed to a phone is saying: "*Doko doko?*" She looks up and around. Another girl comes into view doing much they same. Eventually their eyes meet. They squeal and run towards each other.

An *obasan* is approaching unsteadily on her bike. The pavement is narrow. Instead of applying the brakes she jumps off the bike.

It is a long deep escalator. One person, perhaps from out of town, is standing on the right-hand side. A long queue forms behind her because everyone is too polite to tell her to stand on the left.

I am standing back a step or two and scanning the shelf at the supermarket. From the corner of my eye I notice someone is hesitating. Then he hurries past with his hand apologetically raised, and his head down in an effort not to cut my line of vision. The excessive courtesy of this is delightfully cute.

There is a little ritual that I see in public toilets. A man in a suit is washing his hands at the sink while holding a handkerchief in his mouth. He shakes his hands precisely twice before drying them on the handkerchief.

It is a sunny clear day. I glance up at an apartment building and futons hang from nearly every balcony.

5 Tokyo Vistas

From one, there is the thwump thwump sound of someone beating the dust out.

A man stands alone on a train platform. He takes his umbrella and practices his golf swing.

Two friends are standing on a train when a single seat becomes available. The one who eventually takes the seat offers to hold her friend's bag. I never saw that touching little gesture in any other country.

Aah Japan.

6
Mr Manners and Me

A good many Japanese imagine the classic gentleman to be something like this: he is English, dresses in a suit and possibly carries an umbrella. Perhaps he is a lawyer in London or maybe he just dabbles in the markets. Perhaps James Bond—tall, good looking and with a sophisticated taste in drinks—springs to mind?

Actually, I have met the perfect gentleman. He is an unprepossessing, middle-aged Japanese man who runs a small business, specializing in bolts, near my house. The day I met him he gave a performance of such manners that words sprang to mind I more normally associate with ice skaters: "grace" and "apparent effortlessness".

I met the man with the perfect manners because the bolt that held my saddle in place had snapped completely in two as I rode my bicycle. I spent a fruitless hour at a DIY store trying to fix it. I begged a cycle repair shop to do something, but they didn't have the right bolt.

So I ended up at Mr Manners' shop holding up the two pieces of a big thick bolt, with a pleading look. If I

6 MR MANNERS AND ME

were in Britain, I would now be bracing for the following comments: "How the bloody hell did you do that?" Then: "Here, Dave, come and look at what this clown has done." Then: "We only sell bulk, mate."

Instead my Japanese Mr Manners looked at the bolt, then looked up at me and delivered the perfect reply: "*Kega nakatta?*" ("Were you hurt at all?") It's funny how a few words from a stranger can change your day. Actually, I wasn't hurt. But I had had a nasty shock, falling off my bike late at night and confused as to what had happened. Now, someone made it a lot better with a little bit of sympathy.

I also had a useless bike. I think it is the apogee of good manners to try to help people in distress. Mr Manners could have quite reasonably just sold me a bolt and sent me on my way. Instead, he set about trying to put my saddle back together.

It was a tricky job with little space to work in—and a confusing array of pieces to fit together. First, the bolt wouldn't go in. Then, when we finally got it in, we discovered the new bolt was a few centimeters too long. So out it came. At one stage, I dropped everything all over the floor. Then, when we finally got the bolt in, we realized we had fixed a part on backwards. Mr Manner's patience was equal to all these setbacks.

In the middle of this half-hour struggle, the phone in the shop rang. Mr Manners' wife informed the caller that he was busy with a customer. I don't know who called, but he very likely wanted more than to buy a single bolt. It wouldn't have been at all unreasonable for Mr Manners to ask me to wait while he took the call. But Mr Manners doesn't work like that; my petty problem took priority.

Many readers may have already guessed what happened after my bike was fixed, but even after many years in Japan it still amazed me. Mr Manners declined to accept any kind of payment, making light of what he had done and, for good measure, insisting I take the Allen key in case the bolt became loose.

I suppose the bolt and the key together might have only cost him a few yen. You could argue that he was in the shop anyway and I wasn't taking him away from another job. But I don't see it like that. I never met a lawyer who gives his expertise away gratis. Mr Manners runs a specialist shop and I couldn't have fixed the bike alone. He could have charged me and I wouldn't have thought it at all unreasonable. After all, he made my bike usable again.

Mr Manners must have known that I am not likely

6 Mr Manners and Me

to be coming back with a big order next week. He helped me out for the very best reason: because he is a gentleman. It was an act of generosity of spirit, the likes of which I have experienced many times in Japan.

In Osaka, in my first few weeks in Japan, I bought a bottle of beer at an off-license and asked the shop owner to open it. Instead, he gave me a bottle opener. Fourteen years on, I still have it attached to my key fob not just for practical reasons but as a reminder of this act of kindness.

Perhaps Japanese take this kind of thing for granted. But I feel in Japan a sense of community still prevails, kept alive in part by small local stores.

The thing about good manners is that they are contagious. I believe that every time a person is exposed to such courtesy it inspires him to try to match that standard. The reverse is true as well. In the cities of England today, I feel there is a downward spiral and that bad manners and bad language are becoming the norm. Such things are unquantifiable, of course. But I am far from alone in being struck by the overall level of courtesy in Japan compared to Britain. And I know that it makes a huge difference in your quality of life when you are exposed to good manners rather than bad.

For one day, at least, people did meet a tall English gentleman. It was me, trying to behave towards others in the same way that I had just been treated by Mr Manners. Old ladies blocking my way received patient smiles instead of scowls. A shop owner in Ueno had a customer courteously ask how business was, and then patiently listen to his story about he had once been in a newspaper. And Mr and Mrs Manners received a small packet of strawberries, which they tried to refuse. But all these courtesies were merely a reflection of the greatness of Mr Manners, in his unspectacular way a hero for our times.

7
"Made in Japan" Inventions

What are the five greatest Japanese inventions?

A lot of people might start talking about Walkman or the VHS or even the "just-in-time" manufacturing system, whatever that may be. I think they are barking up the wrong tree.

The truly great inventions are often not considered "inventions", but are ideas that seep into our culture and lives so thoroughly we don't notice them. The weekend, for example. Who decided that we should have two days off out of seven? There is nothing in our biology or even our theology that compels it. We made it up out of nowhere. People who have weekends off may take it for granted (unless it is threatened). People who don't have weekends off fantasize about it. The weekend is simply a brilliant idea.

Japan, I think, is full of brilliant ideas both large and small.

Perhaps the most obvious is *hanami*. Just as it becomes warm enough to sit outside, Japan has a nationwide sit-outside party. After a long winter, it is wonderfully therapeutic. And the blooming of the cherry trees is an act of scheduling genius. I sometimes wonder whether Japanese fixed their new intake of students and company employees to the *hanami* season so that everyone can start off with a session of "bonding through booze". It is also the perfect introduction to company life for new boys. To be told "sit there and keep a space for us until work finishes" must enable them to grasp in a single moment how hierarchy works—and how the talents of newcomers are deployed.

Funnily enough, fond as I am of drinking, it isn't the drink that I like about *hanami*. My pet hates include drinking in the daytime, enforced drinking, drinking to deliberate excess and shouting loudly. Visit Ueno Park at *hanami* time and I think you will see my point.

I think *hanami* has all got too far away from the actual "looking at the blossoms", which are genuinely spectacular. Perhaps I can suggest a new drinking game to restore the balance: before each new drink you must seek out a different kind of *sakura* tree. I think even an amateur can locate five or six varieties in a decent-sized park. And for the determined drinker, there are hundreds of different types in existence, I hear.

7 "Made in Japan" Inventions

My personal favourite Japanese invention is the *sentō* (public bath). It strikes me as the near perfect product. *Sentō* dispense cleanliness and relaxation at hundreds of spots across Tokyo and all over Japan. In summer it is ideal for wiping off the grime of the day before you head out for the evening. In winter it warms you up.

In many of the small and medium cities of the world, such facilities would hardly be needed as you can pop home between a day's shopping and a night out. But in Tokyo most of us live too far away from the places we work and play.

The same is true in London, but it is too late to build public baths where they don't already exist. Economically it doesn't work—not to mention the cultural hurdles that would need to be overcome.

So I consider the *sentō* a unique blessing of Japanese life. But, bizarrely, most Japanese don't realize it. It amazes me how many young people have never been to a *sentō*. Many times I have gone to visit a *sentō*, only to find it has closed since my 2002 *sentō* map was made.

It may just be a failure of marketing. I see *onsen* facilities that charge 2,000 yen are full, but 430 yen *sentō* are used only by the elderly. Yet many are similar in quality to *onsen*, with herb baths, saunas, bubbling baths, massage baths and glorious high ceilings and painted murals.

Perhaps we should advertise the *sentō* as the "portable bath", the washing equivalent of the Walkman. I mean it allows you to enjoy a soak when you feel like it, pretty much anywhere in town. Or perhaps the *sentō* should be compared to a bar. Rather than bathe (or drink) at home, you can enjoy first-class facilities, and mingle and chat. But personally I tell my friends the *sentō* is the perfect way to pass the "dead time" that so often occurs between six and seven. It's the time when it is too early to start drinking or have dinner, but you've finished at the shops or the museum. The *sentō* is the perfect place to refresh and get ready for the rest of the day.

In any case, whenever I have a friend from England they don't need to be sold on the idea. They are always curious about *sentō* from having read their guidebooks. And they always become fans after one visit.

Dear reader, perhaps you haven't thought about it but the book you hold in your hand is a brilliant invention. No, I am not claiming my words are genius—but the *shinsho* and *bunkobon* format itself. I thought so the moment I first saw these small, cheap

7 "Made in Japan" Inventions

paperbacks. Building a book collection in the UK was an expensive business. Publishers devoted their energies to adding value (or "adding cost" as I always call it) with artistic covers, perfect binding, new forewords, new designs and—most irritatingly—larger books with larger typeface. At some stage, the book stopped being about the words and thoughts inside, and became a product in itself, something that is supposed to be beautiful.

This meant, firstly, that the book became too big to fit in your pocket and, secondly, that it is too valuable to lug around on trains where it could get damaged. And it is costly for avid readers to assemble a collection.

I gave a silent round of applause when I first saw the range of work available in a Japanese bookshop at low prices and in such straightforward formats.

But then, I think Japanese are good in general at presenting products in the right way. Can I list "folding and wrapping things nicely" as a great Japanese cultural asset? Certainly it's something that still amazes me about Japan.

Again, it's the cliché about Japanese being good with their hands, but sometimes clichés reveal great truths. Japanese are certainly more dexterous than me. Among my proudest moments is when I learned how to turn the paper sleeve from my disposable chopsticks into an improvised *hashi-oki* (chopstick rest). Then I learned how to tie a knot in a plastic bag from the supermarket so that later, when I want to use it as a bin-liner, all I have to do is pull the ends to open it up.

So you can imagine how far I am from being able to invent something like the *onigiri* (rice ball) wrappers that keep the rice and seaweed apart until you pull tabs 1, 2 and 3. I marvel at paper-wrapped goods where the folds move into each other so logically and efficiently. It reminded me of my first visit to a Japanese castle (Himeji), and how my guide explained that Japanese carpenters worked to conceal all the joints.

When I was at school I loathed art. My teachers called me a philistine. Perhaps they were right, but I prefer to think I was rebelling against something in the art that I was being shown. Mona Lisa stirred me not, nor does it today. I feel a spasm of distaste when I look at portraits of Dutch merchants whose names we would not remember were they not recorded in paint. I didn't get Picasso or Kandinsky, except as background art for a certain type of restaurant.

But Hiroshige and Hokusai immediately appealed

7 "Made in Japan" Inventions

to me. I am no art critic but my amateur analysis is that the process is what makes the art. Printing with woodblocks enabled hundreds or thousands of copies of the same work. So the artists worked not for a single client, nor for some vain rich man, nor for the greater glory of god, nor even in pursuit of some kind of pure individual expression. They excelled in their craft, but they attempted to create art that would sell by the thousands.

As such, they produced landscapes that people knew: the temple at Asakusa, the bridges by which people crossed the Sumida, the Ryogoku fireworks people flocked to see . . . It is easy to find a work of art representing, say, the area where you live or some park you often visit. Sometimes, the passage of time has not made the place unrecognizable, such as with prints of Shinobazu pond in Ueno Park or Horikiri Shobu-en (Iris Garden). Other times, they have changed beyond belief. It is hard today to envisage that there was a waterfall at Oji, or that areas that now teem with people were once fields.

The colours of woodblock prints are immediately striking; the designs have immediate clarity. They form a record of their times—or at least a record of what people were fascinated by. In these *ukiyo-e* prints we see how foreigners mingled among Japanese in the 19th century. We see how trains passed by rickshaws. We see firemen, geisha and actors—figures whom the general public idolized, not just popes and saints.

Another problem with great art is that one can never own it. Humans are acquisitive creatures and we form a special connection with the things we own. Today one can buy a decent *ukiyo-e* for under 10,000 yen, or even a superb edition of a Hiroshige masterpiece for less than a year's salary. A year's salary wouldn't buy you a square inch of a Van Gogh.

Sometimes people say the Japanese are good imitators, that they just take ideas from overseas and make them a bit better. Nothing wrong with doing that, I think. But it is too simplistic. I see the Japanese as great innovators, even if they don't realize it themselves.

8
The Not-Lost Decade

Standard wisdom has it that Japan has been mired in recession for some 15 years. This has been called, with increasing inaccuracy, the "lost decade". Japan's self-confidence has crumbled as its once all-conquering economy has faltered. The bicycle, which worked wonderfully while it propelled forward, has come to a halt.

Personally, I think of the same period as golden years for Japan. Any good Englishman will tell you that the two most important things in life are football and beer (though there is some debate about the order of importance). In my opinion, in those same 15 years Japan has gone from being a hopeless underperformer in both categories to being a serious contender.

For a Brit, one of the great joys in life is tasting a new beer. And one of the great fears is of somehow ending up in a country where the beer is awful. So it was with a mixture of excitement and trepidation that I flew to Japan in 1992.

My first impression of Japanese beer was good. I liked the exotic names and the unusual designs—on the cans and bottles—of unfamiliar gods and mythical beasts. I liked the rich, autumn leaves on the seasonal, limited edition beer. My first taste (Kirin, as it happens) was no disappointment; a fine, clean lager and no mistake.

But the euphoria didn't last. I began to ask why did every beer cost the same? Why did they have exactly the same alcohol content? Why do *izakaya* sell hundreds of different foods and dozens of sakes but only one beer? And, most importantly, why did the beers all taste the same? In blind testing how many people can tell Suntory from Sapporo? To a palate used to beers as diverse as bitters, ales, stouts and lagers, telling two Japanese beers apart is like telling ocean grey paint from military grey. Once, in a desperate bid to drink something other than lager, I bought a can of Mitsuya Cider. When I realized that in Japan "cider" isn't an apple-based beer, I nearly wept.

I planned to get hold of some homebrew equipment and concoct my own porters and bitters. I would hold "batch-ready" parties, at which Japanese friends would initially be suspicious of these strange, room temperature English beers but would soon be converted and wait impatiently for the next cycle. Then I was told that it was illegal in Japan to home brew proper beer—as vile a law against freedom as any I have ever heard of.

My theory is that beer reflects the country that produces it. Australian heat produces bland, thirst-quenching suds. Freezing Belgian monasteries produce complex, heady brews. Japan, I generalized, was a country of numbing uniformity—where people the length and breadth of the country were forced to accept the same standardized product, where money couldn't buy you choice and individual taste was considered a character flaw. I thought it typical of how Japanese government worked, with big companies protected by legislation specifically designed to prevent competition from start-ups.

Things worked after a fashion: after all, Japanese beer was not bad. But different foods and different occasions call for different beers. The great beer critic Michael Jackson (no, not *that* Michael Jackson—this one was a bearded Englishman) once wrote that, if banished to an uninhabited island: "I would want a Bavarian wheat beer to quench my thirst on a hot day, a Bohemian lager to accompany the fish I would catch, a British ale to go with the wild animals I would barbecue and a barley wine to intoxicate me when I longed for escape."

Long ago, I researched, Japan had been home to scores of little breweries. Even today, one sometimes hears of Kabuto Beer, Sakura beer or the Spring Valley brewery. Others are almost completely forgotten: Maruko beer from "Kitakatsushika in Musashino" or Kujaku beer from Osaka. But by the time I reached Japan all this diversity had been lost in favour of four brewers making interchangeable beers. Tragically, even the two imported beers one could most easily find, Budweiser and Heineken, were also two of the least inspiring—their presence a tribute only to their global marketing clout.

In Japan, beers seem to sell not so much on variety or originality as marketing, advertising and distribution (words belonging to businessmen not drinkers). For example, the term "Super Dry" seems so obviously invented by marketing men. I doubt any brewer said: "Hey let's come up with a beer with as little flavour as possible." I have drunk worse beers than Super Dry. Indeed, it goes reasonably well with delicate-tasting Japanese food and spicy food. But as a stand-alone drink it's so bland as to barely exist. In fact, the pint-drinker struggles with any of the standard Japanese beers; the high gas content causes him to blow up like a balloon after three.

8 The Not-Lost Decade

But things have changed. Deregulation has heralded what Mr Jackson called the "beer revolution" in Japan. He has praised how hundreds of small brewers sprung up here from the mid-1990s, even as big concerns buy up the diminishing number of independent brewers in Europe. He has lauded Japan's boldness in daring to brew traditional British beers such as pale ales.

Two Japanese brewers that stand out are Koedo Beer from Kawagoe and Yokohama Beer. Both have produced a laudable range of traditional and original beers. Both have resisted putting their prices at levels where they can only be bought as *omiyage* or occasional treats. In the superb brew-restaurant Umaya no Shokutaku in Yokohama, you can taste the whole range of Yokohama beers surrounded by the smell of the fermenting hops. The Chimney chain of *izakaya* across Tokyo has brought us premium beers at decent prices. The big brewers themselves have been forced to bring out more experimental beers.

I can't be pessimistic about a country that can create a whole new culture of beer in a few years. I admire the people who can look at big companies, with their marketing millions, and decide to take a bit of their market. In every glass I sip, I sense the sheer inventiveness, the good taste and the wonderful diversity of the Japanese.

Japan's lack of a footballing culture was a major worry too. I could see that Japanese school kids played football well. In terms of fitness, they were clearly miles ahead of most English. Indeed, seeing the way high school clubs trained daily even during the summer holiday I actually feared they may be playing too much.

But generally Japan was a barren football desert. I wonder if people remember what it was like before there was a professional league in Japan and an international team worth following? Can you imagine the horror a European experiences coming to a country where more people follow the World Series than the World Cup?

Every country should have its eccentric individual sport. I enjoy sumo as much as the next man. In England we have cricket, a bizarre game that can drag on for five days, including breaks for tea, and still end in a draw. But, alongside its novelty sport, every proper country needs football. Baseball is no substitute, being a sport only of the American commonwealth. How do they have the nerve to call it a World Series when only two countries participate?

(If the two countries were America and Japan it would at least be inter-continental.)

Today the standard of play in the J. League is immeasurably higher than in 1993. Japan is now well placed to grace the World Cup every four years and, I believe, can be more than also-rans. A number of Japanese players have done well in the tough leagues of Europe. Not just in terms of talent, but attitude and application, have Japanese players excelled. I look at Junichi Inamoto who has persevered through long difficult spells: at Arsenal (where he never got a chance), injury, a loan to the rather obscure Cardiff, a move to Fulham, then unglamorous West Bromwich Albion and demotion. And yet he has achieved some great things, not least scoring a winning goal against Manchester United.

But for me an equally important transformation has been in crowd culture. At early J. League games people didn't seem to know quite how to act or what to enjoy. Marketing men tried to show them. The result was comical. I remember a lackluster match in Osaka when the crowd "oohed" with delight as a hapless defender ran out of options and simply punted the ball as far as he could upfield. Even more alarming were the "cheerphones", which you blew into when your team had the ball. Then the other team got the ball and the opposition fans blew theirs. It reminded me of the sound of a paper comb makes—an improvised musical instrument for an English sing-a-long, made by wrapping a comb in paper and blowing into it.

There was a lame and misguided attempt to borrow a fan culture from Brazil. The clubs had Latino-sounding official songs. Fans wore face paint and some brought samba drums. It struck me as a horrible mismatch.

But then Japan began to evolve its own approach. It seemed to take the best from England—the passion and commitment—without the manic anger and potential for violence. It added in a Japanese element of organization: the cheering squads which practice for the games. Football in Japan is probably more family-oriented and has more female fans than in any other country. I like the way you can buy beer at the stadium, but there isn't much drunkenness. I like the way the fans stay behind their team even if they are awful (though I find it hard to do myself). Most of all, I like the way so many Japanese have, in the space of a few years, turned into connoisseurs of the game, learning to love the great soap opera in all its fascinating detail.

I have met Japanese who support West Ham—one of the favourite second teams for Englishmen. I have met people can tell me who is in the Barcelona line-up. People will ask me about the new Arsenal stadium. In other words, there is lots of football to talk and lots of beer to be drunk. Japan's cultural miracle.

9
Turning Japanese

"**Turning** Japanese. I think I'm turning Japanese, I really think so . . . "

These are words from a pop song from the early 1980s, which today is remembered by just about everyone I know. Partly it's so memorable because of the absurdly infectious tune, but also the outrageousness of the idea. Turning Japanese? I don't think so. East is east and west is west . . .

And yet, one does find oneself becoming Japanese. Probably not in the ways you might expect. I wouldn't, for example, consider changing nationality. I am unlikely to become a fanatical believer in Shinto. Ridiculously, before I first went to Japan, I worried that I would "get rusty" at English through speaking "and thinking" in Japanese. Now, I can say with confidence that it is a lot harder to get "polished" at your second language than rusty in your native tongue.

Rather, I find myself picking up all kinds of Japanese mannerisms. A fellow British correspondent notes that even in English he finds himself starting

9 Turning Japanese

any request with the words: "I know you're very busy but . . . ", a phrase that is not usually necessary in the UK. We also joke about being "severely scolded" by our editors; using an English verb that summons up images of naughty children, but which is the only way to translate the Japanese *shikaru*. And I can get very upset if a shop assistant tells me something is "sold out" without a preceding "I am very sorry but . . . ", or some equivalent of "*mōshi wake arimasenga*".

Then there are certain customs that you just can't shake off, because they simply make such sense. I don't think I am the only Brit in Japan unable to go back to the way we used to bathe, sitting there in the soap slime. Two of my old school friends in England, having lived in Japan, insist on people taking their shoes off before entering the house.

Curiously, so do my parents and older sister, none of whom have ever been to Japan. I think this may be the result of slow proselytism on my part. Over the years I have seen how my family got more and more interested in the bits and bobs I sent them from Japan. I don't mean expensive things—just anything with that hint of Japanese aesthetics that marks it out from the usual. Pride of place on one of my sister's shelves goes to a "*free cup*" that I bought at a 100 yen store.

My grandmother was very fond of a *fukin* that I sent her, just a bit of cloth with a print of a gourd in deep blue. I tried to explain she could use it to dry the dishes, but she kept it on the mantelpiece.

It's strange that Japanese aesthetics is instantly understandable in this way. Becauce living here has made me less able to communicate with my countrymen.

For one thing, I stopped being able to use current slang. There was a weird moment back in 1997 when anything that went wrong was said to have "gone pear-shaped". The first time I heard it, I burst out laughing at the originality of the expression. In fact, in the brief time since its creation the phrase had become universal, so my friend thought I was laughing at his misfortune as he explained how everything had gone pear-shaped.

The last time I went to England I discovered that "pants" is the new way to say "rubbish", as in "Bolton are a pants football team". However, by the time I summoned up the courage to use the word, six months later, I found it was already outdated.

Meanwhile, my friends can detect which words I have been picking up from Japan. I overuse the word "boom", apparently. Then I try to insert local words

9 Turning Japanese

into my stories, like "there was a table of *ojisan* next to us . . . " and "it was a case of *shō ga nai*". One day, I fear I will only be able to talk seamlessly with other Englishmen who have lived in Japan. (I must guard the friendship of this small group.)

When I think of trains, too, I am becoming awfully Japanese. In England a train timetable is largely a work of fiction, used only to give an indication of how long it should be between trains. But after a year in Japan you find yourself getting confused if the train is 90 seconds late. If there is no announcement, you instinctively check to see if your watch is wrong.

I never thought I would bother with this, but I head for the carriage that is best for making the connection at Akihabara, or for jumping the escalator at Meguro. In England, it isn't worth it because the train is only about five carriages long. And anyway the driver stops at a random spot anywhere along the platform.

I may be wrong but I think people have a capacity to be annoyed that is not really related to how genuinely annoying things are. In England, a train passenger is guilty of bad manners if he starts a fight or sprays graffiti. In Japan, I find myself thinking ill of a person whose Walkman is too loud. (I would tap him on the shoulder, but his anti-social tendencies means he may be aggressive.)

I have even picked up some Japanese obsessions that I used to find tiresome. When I have visitors from home I find it fascinating to make them try *nattō* and *ume boshi*, those strange Japanese foodstuffs. And I watch compulsively to see if they are putting the burnable and non-burnable rubbish into the right bins.

You stop noticing things that amazed you when you first came. You cease to read the daft messages in poor English written on Japanese clothing. One day, you find you are able to hold conversation, without laughing, with someone wearing one of those anti-allergy face masks.

Your perceptions change subtly without you noticing. Instead of feeling scared about getting mugged because you are carrying a whopping 50,000 yen in your wallet, you think you need to go the bank because you are running low. You see a forty-year-old building and think it is old. Then you see a hundred-year-old building of little architectural merit, and of no great beauty, but desperately want it to be preserved.

The way you look at people changes. It may not be

9 Turning Japanese

a nice thing to say, but the first time I found myself surrounded by Japanese (on a bus at the airport) I thought they all looked the same. It may be because a white person instinctively looks first at things like eye colour, hair colour, shape of nose and whether the hair is curly, wavy or straight. All these things tend to be quite similar in Japanese. It didn't take long before I realized that Japanese people no more look alike than English people do. But what I never expected was that one day I would be able to look at a Japanese person and think he resembles a friend from home. (If I told that to the friend in question, he would believe I had gone mad.)

I used to dream of London pubs. I loved the way you could wander around and strike up conversations with people. I loved the low prices and didn't mind waiting at the bar. I hated, absolutely bloody hated, the way in *izakaya* they would seat you at a table not of your own choosing and expect you to stay there. Once, my friend sparked up a conversation with some students at the next table and was told by the waiter not to do so. The reason? The students were on an all-you-can-drink *nomihōdai* deal and the staff were worried we might sneak beer off them.

But somewhere along the way I changed. Now I

hate having to lurk hopefully at the bar for service, when I could be chatting with my friend. That's what I went there for, after all. Now, I don't really enjoy standing to drink, and think it's not quite civilized to booze without food. I still miss the quality and range of beer in English pubs. But somewhere along the way I reached the point where I think that a decent *izakaya* gets the nod over the pub experience. When I was a poor student, nothing bothered me more than the *otōshi*. (400 yen for a bit of reconstituted fish I never ordered!) These days, I consider it a blessing when it arrives. I am usually starving, and if I am with a group of Japanese I know how long it will take before anything gets ordered.

Then there are some customs I really wish I could acquire. Japanese patience, for one. I am sure I look funny muttering angrily and gesturing at the elevators, as all three move in unison away from me, stopping at every floor on the way up, then every floor on the way back down to me. I have sometimes wondered whether it is possible to identify the gene that makes Japanese able to wait silently.

Sometimes I've wondered whether I would be able to pass as an Englishman anymore. I got badly caught out two years ago when one of my editors spotted me

9 Turning Japanese

putting cream into my espresso. Apparently, only "we Japanese" do that. Then, one embarrassing day, I got off the phone in England and my sister told me I had been bowing as I said my goodbyes and thank yous. She looked at me with a mixture of amusement and despair, at her brother who was turning Japanese.

9.5
Every Day is April Fool's

"Why do so many Japanese wear those face masks?" asked my friend Trevor. "They are doctors and nurses. In Japan they have to wear them until they get home," I answered.

"Why do they play those little jingles on the platform?" "To cheer people up. Stops them from jumping onto the tracks," a helpful voice chips in.

"Why do the announcements on the train go on so long? What are they saying?" asks Trevor. "He's reading out the news for passengers. Often it's too crowded to open up your newspaper."

It pains me that Japanese consider this kind of joke to be *ijime* (bullying). For us Brits, the "wind-up" is a way of life: the funniest (if not the highest) form of humour. A great wind-up will be lovingly recalled among friends for years. A true artist can deliver a hopelessly unbelievable line without giving the game away.

Can't you at least try it? Just imagine it's April Fool's Day every day. I am sure you'll get the hang of it. You also have the ideal opportunity in the form of visitors

9.5 EVERY DAY IS APRIL FOOL'S

from overseas, who find Japan so confusing and will look to you trustingly for guidance. Perhaps you could wind up a Brit like my dear friend Trevor?

Tell him everyone from taxi drivers to policemen speaks English, and that Japanese only pretend not to understand because of the culture of modesty. "Just keep talking to them and eventually they will answer."

Tell him to meet you at "the ticket gates at Shinjuku station". Don't be any more specific than that. Warn him not to bump into anyone at the station or on the platform as most Japanese are good at martial arts. Tell him there's no need to pile onto a crowded train in the morning. "Wait for the next one, which should be along in a few minutes. If that one is crowded too, then wait for the next one."

Tell your visitor *yaki-imo* baked potato vans are *uyoku* (Japanese nationalists), singing of their love for a divine emperor. He may have heard of "sound trucks" and it'll be easy to trick him. (But please don't tell him the *uyoku* are selling potatoes. A wind-up shouldn't be life-threatening.)

If he is a vegetarian, take him for *udon*. Tell him he can't have *kitsune udon* because *kitsune* means fox. Recommend *tanuki udon* instead. Make sure he drains every drop of the "delicious soup". On the way home tell him you have just "remembered" that *tanuki* is the Japanese word for raccoon dog.

Teach him some useful Japanese, such as the names of convenience stores (*nana-juichi*) and how to ask the time (*ojikan arimasuka?*) Explain that the politest way to ask a lady on a date is to invite her for tea (*cha nomimasenka?*)

Tell him that *hashi* means both "bridge" and "chopsticks" depending on intonation. Then say it exactly the same way twice and ask him to learn the difference.

Confuse him by translating things that don't need to be translated. Tell him *Momo-iro Hyo* is a popular cartoon character here. Feign confusion when he calls the same character "Pink Panther". Call *okonomiyaki* "Japanese pizza" and *onigiri* a "Japanese sandwich". Then completely bamboozle him by calling pizza an "Italian-style *okonomiyaki*".

If he should be invited to a Japanese house, advise him it is good manners to finish every drop of beer in his glass. Mention in passing that if someone refills it, he must drain that too. When he comes back drunk, tell him not to drink so much.

Translate place names into English so that he thinks it will be nice to go to Kawaguchi to see the source of the Arakawa, and Uguisudani to listen to the birds sing.

Warn him against taking photographs inside shrines for religious reasons. If he asks why Japanese are doing it, tell him they are "heretics".

Everyone knows Japan has very strict manners. Tell him it's rude to break eye contact when bowing. Encourage him to return every bow from staff at department stores and restaurants. But mention that taking shoes on and off is optional, and just because Japanese do it he doesn't have to.

Tell him it is polite to call someone "*-san*", very polite to use "*-sama*" and a special mark of respect to say "*-chan*". But don't put it in writing as this will make it hard to deny later.

Send him to the barber. But don't warn him that barbers in Japan do shoulder and neck massages. If he says something about it later, look confused and suggest: "Well, you are quite good looking."

Tell him Tora-san is the "Japanese James Bond". Invite him round to the house to watch three classic Tora-san films back to back. If he manages to sit through them suggest: "Tomorrow we get started on *Tsuri Baka Nisshi*."

Take him to Asakusa and laughingly ask him if he

can guess what the local children call the Asahi Beer Hall building. When he gives the usual answer, tell him with a straight face: "They call it the Flame Building."

Bring him to the Kamiya Bar and treat him to a glass of Denki Bran so that he can experience something unique to Japan. After he has drunk it, say: "I never touch the stuff. Tastes awful."

Perhaps by now your friend is thinking of leaving Japan. Tell him you intend to give him some pot pourri. Get him *katsuo bushi* "fish flakes" instead.

Buy something heavy and give it to him at the airport. Pretend it's a Japanese custom based on an ancient belief that a weighty present will bring the recipient back one day. For good measure, make it something that he can easily buy at home—a 2kg packet of spaghetti, say.

Tell him to come back soon. Recommend June, "before the summer heat".

10
Loving an Unlovely City

To say that I love Japan is like saying that I love myself. It is not an unconditional kind of love. I see endless room for improvement. I find bitter fault at times. But at the end of the day it is unthinkable that I would actually cut it from my heart. If someone were to criticize it unfairly I would feel an overwhelming urge to defend it vigorously.

But it took me almost ten years to decide that I liked Tokyo. It is not, in my view, an easy city to enjoy. I have known expat bankers who loved it instantly. But I cannot help thinking they are in love with the pampered lifestyle they live, with apartments costing 700,000 yen per month and housekeepers. I assume that guest workers of Japanese ancestry love it too, because it offers employment and the chance to live in a place not wrecked by drugs and crime—things not guaranteed for poor people even in developed countries.

But I, and probably you, fall somewhere in between. And Tokyo isn't an easy city for us to enjoy. For a start, it must be among the most physically ugly cities in the world.

For many Western visitors the neon glare is what strikes them first, and many people will speak of the intense "energy" of Asian cities. Yes, for a week's holiday you may be struck by the sense of anticipation that bright lights stir up, especially with all that exotic lettering. But after a while, the glare just becomes a kind of visual pollution. It is the equivalent of walking down a market street and having traders shout at you to look at their wares. It is tiresome and intrusive.

The paucity of park space is depressing to anyone who has ever lived in London or New York, especially with Tokyo's lack of private gardens. I felt something close to grief when I realized that grass does not just grow naturally wherever there is a patch of land free. I considered lush, green grass a kind of natural force, like gravity or water. I just assumed all developed countries had it. Certain of the parks in Tokyo, such as Kiyosumi Shirakawa or Rikugien, are a delight. But these parks are few and small for a city of Tokyo's scale. You don't just "stumble across" them or stroll over from the office during lunchtime. They are not part of the fabric of the city.

I took much consolation in the fact that Japan was blessed with mountains and sea views which, in cities

10 Loving an Unlovely City

such as Kobe, amply compensate. But in Tokyo little use is made of features such as the canals, the Sumida and the sea. There are some unspoiled spots by the Sumida that the Construction Ministry forgot to destroy. But sadly few people in Tokyo appreciate and enjoy these resources.

Development has crushed much of the character of Japanese cities. Am I alone in hating the moment you walk out of a station, in some new city, only to find it looks exactly the same as every other city? There is the same huge traffic rotunda that requires pedestrians to walk to one set of traffic lights, then another, before you hit the same *ekimae* (next-to-the-station) stores that you see everywhere. Your first sight is of traffic. You have to delve into each city for some time to discover its charms.

It seems Japan is in the process of wiping out any areas that have some remaining character. The case of Shimo-Kitazawa, scheduled for just this kind of "redevelopment", is saddening. I am glad that many Japanese care enough to oppose this "de-characterisation", but saddened that they have almost no hope of succeeding.

I used to sit on the steps of the Eros statue in Piccadilly and enjoy the prospect along Shaftesbury

Avenue. No view is more pleasing to the eye. Though the street is prime real estate, the elegant buildings have been preserved even as commerce came to dominate. At ground level are all the stores and pubs. The street curves and the buildings sweep along with it in the most delightful manner. And, of course, the buildings are of the same height and style. You do not find, in the manner of Tokyo, a noodle shop between two skyscrapers, or a pachinko parlour set next to a historic shrine.

I wonder if anyone in any Japanese city has a view that they love in the way I love Shaftesbury Avenue. I can think of some nice spots, such as the Bandai Bridge in Niigata over the splendid Shinano River, or the pleasant Japanese garden inside the Meguro Gajoen Hotel complex. But I would have loved to wander through Marunouchi in its "Londontown" incarnation, when it was all red brick. I look longingly at old woodblock prints of Tokyo and wish that even a hint of that character remained.

When it comes to old buildings, I am something of a fundamentalist. I cannot bear to see one torn down unless it is ugly, commercially non-viable *and* about to be replaced with something of greater beauty or merit or need. I don't understand how the Finance Ministry could so casually tear down the Shoda house in Gotanda, where Empress Michiko grew up, despite the laudable campaign started by local people to preserve it.

This little piece of history was cynically destroyed on the very day the invasion of Iraq began—a timing guaranteed to ensure the news did not garner media attention. The truth is, if the house were in London, its architectural merits alone would not make it worth preserving. It was rather an odd concoction; Tudor-style in the Taisho era. But Tokyo suffers from a dreadfully poverty of "old" buildings. In Tokyo, "prewar" is old. In England, we don't use the word "old" for anything from the last century.

I think of those historic Tokyo buildings which met a cruel and unnecessary end. The pagoda in Yanaka was burned down in a lovers' suicide pact in 1957. The splendid 12-story Ryounkaku that stood in Asakusa was damaged by the Kanto earthquake of 1923 and had to be torn down. Since neither met a deserved death, is it unreasonable to suggest restoring them? The latter building is something of an obsession with me. I have loved this bizarre "piece of confection" since I first heard of it. Then I was delighted to hear that it was actually designed by a Briton, William

Kinninmond Burton. Burton was in fact not a trained architect, but rather the engineer who helped build Japan's sewage and water sanitation systems a hundred years ago.

In London, we have seen how recreated buildings can work. Shakespeare's Globe Theatre was destroyed by fire in the 17th century but rebuilt a decade ago, by the efforts of an American, on the south bank of the Thames near where the original stood. Today it is a thriving, living theatre and a tourist attraction.

In Japan, too, we can see a thirst for historic buildings. I think of the old Akarenga Sōko (Red Brick Warehouse) in Yokohama, so wonderfully reborn for the present-day, with shops and restaurants and open space around it. Its location is perfect and the interior has lovely high ceilings. Could Japan not do with a few more of these places?

And yet Tokyo is a remarkable city that grows and grows on you. As I have hinted above, there are the wondrous little corners. I keep a list of "secret places" across Tokyo that I visit when I have the chance. One of the most lovely places to sit and read a book in the afternoon is the riverside park at Etchujima. At this point the Sumida River splits in two and the branches slip by either side of Tsukishima island.

Tokyo is also a wonder for its specialist districts. Many tourists head for Akihabara, once "electric town" but more "anime town" today. It is generous of Tokyo, as one writer put it, to gift Harajuku—several square kilometers of prime real estate—to the youth of Tokyo. Friends from overseas gawp in astonishment at the fashions they see there.

Personally, I prefer "*Obasan* Harajuku", the Sugamo district where old people gather. Some people squeal with delight when they see puppies or little children. For me, it is a certain type of elderly Japanese person. Nothing warms my heart more than a couple holding hands after, I assume, forty years of marriage. Or the sight of elderly women taking tea together and swapping tips on which tonics work. They seem so much more cheerful and healthy than the elderly in Britain, and it gives me great hope. For that matter, they often seem more cheerful than the kids in Harajuku, who seem to be in soulless pursuit of some piece of fashion that they think will make them complete.

The early morning fish market at Tsukiji is, I am assured, a wonder. I believe it, and intend to see it one day. If only they wouldn't hold it so ridiculously early. For us late risers, Tokyo has an even more astonishing market—a whole area devoted to every kind of accessory and hardware needed for kitchens and restaurants. I can think of cities with central fish markets—London for one—but where else is there an equivalent of Kappabashi?

It is not just the fact of its existence. It is the quality and novelty of things you can find there. Many foreigners pause to take pictures of the plastic food samples. The classic shot is the "chopsticks suspended magically in the air, trailing some noodles down to the ramen bowl".

I have bought rice bowls and plates and chopsticks, but my personal fetish is drinking vessels: the "*free cups*" I use for beer, sake cups and sake bottles, and even a wine goblet of such unusual design I struggle to describe it. I calculate that I can drink for a whole month without ever using the same cup twice—and, as you may have guessed by now, I drink more often than once or twice a month.

The residential neighbourhoods of Tokyo hold hidden joys. Every local shopping street is unique. Each *sentō* a little temple to cleanliness. For years I carried a Tokyo *sentō* map, made in 2002, along with my miniature towel and soap, so that I could locate the baths wherever I found myself in the city, whether to warm up or clean away the sweat, to help shed a headache, or to work up a thirst and appetite for the evening ahead. Today, I no longer carry the map as so many of the *sentō* are gone. Instead, I keep an eye open for a local carrying his *sentō* stuff in a little plastic bowl. Asking the locals is better because, as often as not, they will give me the insider knowledge on which *sentō* is best. Sometimes they insist on walking me there.

Which brings me to the great wonder of Tokyo—its people. I cannot think of any city where one is treated with such kindness and courtesy on a routine basis. Where people do not intrude on you, but where striking up conversation is generally easy. And where it is joyously difficult to get into a fight.

I like the way petrol pump attendants bow. I can't say I see the need for a man with a glowing stick to wave you past a hole in the pavement, especially when that hole is already amply marked with traffic cones. But I admire the way he does this job with the diligence and attention of an air traffic controller. I have a special devotion to Tokyo's supermarket ladies. If there were a world ranking for skill and speed at the checkout till, Japan would surely rank first. Such everyday encounters are a constant reminder that people care about their jobs, the community they live in and the people they come into contact with.

For journalists, Tokyo has much to offer. The concentration of business, arts, academia and government in one city makes life more diverse than for my counterparts in, say, Washington DC. I also appreciate how well-informed people are. I am always shy of approaching people for what we call "vox pop", the views of the man-in-the-street on some news story. But when I do stop people, I am almost always impressed to hear some new idea or some carefully balanced view. If only I could get that faithfully into the newspaper.

My friend Richard Lloyd Parry, who has lived in Japan for twelve years and is bureau chief of *The Times*, says the great joy of Tokyo is that whatever he is reporting on, no matter how obscure, somewhere there is a small organisation passionately devoted to that single issue. Often, there are "for" and "against" organisations. If there are people desperately opposed to the use of *waribashi* (disposable chopsticks), there are sure to be people desperately trying to protect them.

An American journalist did a remarkable story about a group of Japanese dedicated to traditional tattoos, desperate to preserve the art and desperate to show that it is not only for yakuza gangsters.

A decade ago a colleague in the US told me he had heard that the Japanese are "mad about the Beat Poets". I doubt if one in ten Japanese know what a Beat Poet is. But I am sure that somewhere, in some appropriate bar, a band of committed fans meet regularly to recite Ginsburg. At the same time, *The New York Times* ran a lengthy piece on the Japanese "boom" in singing gospel. I had never heard of it until then, but of course it was true. Despite the lack of any connection to Christianity or African-American culture, a certain number of young Japanese were pursuing gospel with commendable passion.

My friend visited from England and, on one of our first nights in Tokyo, we chanced across 50 or 60 "Mods", followers of a fashion from the 1960s in England. The Japanese Mods were perfect replicas: Sta-prest trousers, pencil-thin ties, Parka coats, Lambretta bikes with fur tails attached to the upstanding aerial . . . "Wow, Mods are big here still?" he asked. I had never seen them before, nor have I since.

Permit me to go back to the Ryounkaku. I had longed to find out more about this strange building, which was such an emblem of the late Meiji and early Taisho eras. I had seen it portrayed in hundreds of woodblock prints and postcards from the era. Sure enough, I discovered a group of experts: Japanese engineers devoted to remembering Mr Burton's achievements.

Many years ago, an English-language magazine in Japan ran a competition to create a slogan for Tokyo. Many readers were impressed with the entry that called Tokyo "a good place to smoke and drink". But the deserving winner, handwritten in touchingly poor grammar, declared Tokyo a "city of good peoples". As someone who been a resident for over a decade, I have to agree that it is the people that make Tokyo great. If I were to have entered that contest, I might have penned this line: "Tokyo: city of myriad pursuits, and enthusiasm allied to knowledge."

11
Let's Tokyo

This next sentence might not seem to make sense but please bear with me. Precisely because foreign visitors know little about Japan they come here with an impressive amount of knowledge. That is to say, rather than just roll up—as they might do with Paris, already having a reasonable idea of where to go and how to enjoy themselves—for Tokyo, they prepare. It may just be a few hours reading their guidebooks on the airplane, but most seem to be well-primed on arrival.

As a matter of pride—after more than a decade in Tokyo I like to think I am the expert—I have never bought either of the main guidebooks: *Lonely Planet* and *Rough Guide*. But I am aware that they are a formidable obstacle to my ambitions of being hailed by my friends as the "local expert".

From quick glances at borrowed copies, and from the look of familiarity on people's faces when I have suggested outings, I infer that these guidebooks cover not just all the main areas of interest in Japan's big cities and all the main attractions, but are rich in quirky ideas of things to see and do, as well as cultural tips.

I have had friends arrive here already equipped to deal with the vagaries of Japanese bath etiquette. It's no good recommending to them an interesting experience called "*kaitenzushi*"; they will already have marked out the one where they want to eat breakfast after a trip to the Tsukiji Fish Market. When I mention Shibuya, I get the reply: "Yes, we want to get some pictures of that crazy crossing." They know what they are doing.

I hate just to parrot the guidebook. So over the years I have evolved my own alternative little list of suggestions of what to enjoy in Tokyo, which I wish to share with you.

Go for a run along the Sumida River. The best starting point is the Mannenbashi Bridge, where the Sumida meets the Onagigawa canal, and where sits the statue of Matsuo Basho (and, incidentally, the house in Tokyo I would most like to own). Run—or walk—down to Etchujima, around the tip of Tsukishima (which really is a crescent moon shaped island, as the name suggests) and back up the other side. It's about a 5km round trip. En route, you will encounter very few people—and plenty of cormorants playing in the water. The ideal time to run is as evening falls and the Eitaibashi and Harumibashi bridges light up beautifully.

Get into the habit of walking. Buy a pocket map of Tokyo from a 100 yen shop to help you find quiet back streets. Tokyo's public transport is so good people rarely walk, but the hidden cost of trains is that you whiz past (or under) so much.

Try for example taking a morning dip in the temple-like Daikoku Yu *sentō* in Adachi Ward. Then walk all the way to art deco 20 Seiki no Yu ("The 20th Century Baths") in Nihonzutsumi. Stop along the way, as things take your fancy, and by the time you get there another soak may well be in order.

Or start your walk at the Yasuda Teien, a charming little garden in Ryogoku that is free and never crowded. One can sit by the lake with the Kokugikan sumo stadium in the background. The garden has a beautiful collection of stone lanterns and is particularly beautiful in the snow. From there, head down to Kiyosumi Shirakawa Teien, a garden whose charms need no recommendation from me. En route, you may find little *wagashi* sweet stores or a ceramic workshop with a few items on sale at factory prices.

It's a long walk, but it's worth continuing to the "sumo shrine", Tomioka Hachimangu at Monzen

Nakacho. Find the stone *yokozuna* tablet, where the names of the sumo greats are inscribed in bold calligraphy. Then seek out the hand and foot impressions, preserved in stone, of these giant men of sumo. Be awed.

Skip Meiji Shrine and instead go to the Togo Shrine ten minutes' walk away. Here, panels on the walls tell the extraordinary story of Heihachiro Togo's long and eventful life. The garden and pond next to the shrine are a perfect oasis compared to the heaving streets of Harajuku.

There are many things to do "by the way". Every time you go through Hamamatsucho on the Yamanote Line, check out the peeing boy. The endless variety of costumes in which he is dressed is a marvel. It's typical of Japan that a space so small could be turned into a spectacle, and that so much care could be lavished on something so otherwise ordinary.

Or you can visit the cutest little *kōban* (police box) in Tokyo, halfway down the "Monja Street" on Tsukishima.

Buy a bottle of wine and have an evening picnic in Etchujima Park, on the banks of the Sumida overlooking Tsukishima. The *yakata-bune* party boats, all lit up with lanterns, flow past incessantly. The view is better from the river banks than from inside the boats, as well as cheaper.

Drinking beer is crucial to how a holiday is remembered. Many a visitor's fondest memory will be of an *izakaya* where they were treated warmly and enjoyed the company of friends. After extensive research into drinking establishments I can make the following four recommendations.

For atmosphere, it must be the Kamiya Bar in Asakusa, which bills itself as Tokyo's oldest Western-style "bar". Here, you can catch here a glimpse of what Asakusa might have been like when it was the centre of Tokyo life, and the favourite haunt of characters such as Yasunari Kawabata. It's lucky the Kamiya Bar has been there so long, as no one could create it today. Who could devise a combination of low prices and waiters in bow-ties? Its headline product, Denki Bran, tastes vile. Surely it is only drunk out of nostalgia. The Kamiya closes at 10 pm, which is around the time many people feel want to start an evening out. Yet somehow the place works.

For range and quality, you must head to Popeye in Ryogoku. To the best of my knowledge, it has the most extensive selection of Japanese craft beers in the country, including a phenomenal 40 beers on tap. It also has many imported and bottled beers. Smaller than an English pub but with a far wider selection, Popeye is a marvelous antidote to all those *izakaya* that, annoyingly, sell only Asahi Super Dry.

For location and environment, I recommend the roof of the Kudan Kaikan hotel during its long beer garden season, from May to September. There is something strikingly elegant about the building as you enter. This contrasts nicely with the messiness that always follows a grand drinking session here. From the Kudan Kaikan you can look out over the Chidorigafuchi moat and the Showa Kan. It is as pleasant a place to pass a warm night as any I know.

The building itself is historic. Today, it is a guest hotel and wedding facility but it was once the Gunjin Kaikan, used by soldiers of the Imperial Army. Little wonder it is so close to Yasukuni Shrine, which must also be on any tourist's itinerary (not so much the shrine itself, but the appalling Yushukan museum within the grounds, and the lovely garden at the back).

For a solitary beer, nowhere surpasses the Ginza Lion beer hall. Now seventy years old, it has survived war, requisition by the American occupation forces and the development of Tokyo. If I were better with words I could give you a hint of the pleasures of the interior. The beauty is in the mural behind the bar and the stone fountains sitting on the marble bar. It's in the "four seasons" theme on the walls. And in the ornate chandeliers that hang from the gorgeous ceilings. It's actually a waste to go to the Lion with a friend, because you need to stop talking and pay attention to all the visual details.

Buy a one-day pass for the Toden tram—a bargain at 700 yen. It's a sort of trundling time machine, running through all the parts of Tokyo that retain a feel of the past. It is worth stopping at Oji when the brilliant *sakura* of Asukayama Park are in bloom. Stop at Zoshigaya for a walk around the peaceful cemetery, where Soseki Natsume and Lafcadio Hearn are among those buried. Check out the shopping arcade at Minowa.

Museums are a tricky subject in Tokyo. The big museums are not bad, but do not rival the best museums in London or New York. Unless it's raining, it may not be worth spending three hours of a short holiday. But where Japan excels is in fascinating little museums that you can pop into for forty minutes, or even less, while wandering around town. Most cost less than a cup of coffee, or are even free. Does any other country have such interesting micro-museums?

The Meguro Parasitological Museum is perhaps the pick of the bunch. All you ever needed to know about worms but were too squeamish to ask. The Sumo Museum in the Kokugikan is but a single room. But it is free, changes exhibitions regularly and is worth visiting just to stare at the faces of the *yokuzuna* from the past. There is the tiny Basho Memorial Museum, where one can learn a bit about the life of this prolific poet. The museum is near his statue at the Mannenbashi Bridge, which I mentioned above. Or there is the Beer Museum Yebisu in Ebisu Garden Place, where one can learn about brewing and taste some rare brews. The Tobacco and Salt Museum in Shibuya at first confuses. It's as odd a combination as, say, a Coffee and Cheese Museum, until you learn that a state monopoly once controlled both tobacco and salt in Japan. It's fascinating, if only for the amazing collection of cigarette labels. But I still wonder why they have a display of "famous smokers through history" without a corresponding display of "great salt lovers".

If you must go to Ueno Park, then go. Afterwards, pop into the Suigetsu Hotel where you can use the *onsen* facilities for a small sum. It's a great bath, but the real point is to see the beautifully preserved former house of Ogai Mori, which sits in the hotel's inner courtyard.

But for Tokyo's single best-kept secret, head south to Ota Ward. Take in the Ikegami Plum Tree Garden before finding your way round to the splendid Honmonji Temple. The grounds contain many highpoints, but the crowning glory is the hidden Shotoen, a 400-year-old garden where the famous Saigo Takamori and Katsu Kaishu once took tea together. If I were charged 1,000 yen to go in, I would still visit every time I was in the area. But, wonder of wonders, you can enter without paying a penny.

Instead, you must complete a form with twelve questions about Honmonji, the answers to which you can find at various places around the temple complex. It's a brilliant way of restricting access to a few dozen people an hour, as well as rewarding people for taking an interest in the temple. You can often sit for an hour almost alone, just relishing the beauty and silence.

Tokyo is a city of nooks and crannies, of things-to-do too numerous to list. To find them, you need to slow down, enquire and listen. Tokyo is strangely lacking in any single great tourist attraction or perfect photo spot. But, in its numerous surprises and hidden corners, it is among the most diverse and extraordinary cities on earth. Perhaps that's the wonder of it: that after ten years of investigating Tokyo I cannot really claim to be an expert.

12
Two Island Nations

I am standing in Ueno Park and listening to a very strange warbling noise emerging from a Japanese man who is obviously in the grip of intense emotion. Other men, similarly middle-aged, watch with determined concentration.

This, I assume, is *enka*. The sound is so odd, so alien and disagreeable, that I am shocked out of the everyday. For a moment, I am not just walking in the park on a warm spring evening. I am a foreigner in a faraway country, engaging with a completely different culture. I am gripped by the powerful and pleasing sensation that I am a pioneer, boldly living somewhere few Britons could ever live.

At this point, one of the men approaches me and asks me what I think of the music. "Very interesting," I reply. He asks me where I come from. "Aah England. That makes sense," he says. "You see, England and Japan are very alike. It's natural you can appreciate *enka*."

It's an idea I have heard many times: England and Japan are similar. But I doubt I am giving away a state secret if I reveal that on every single occasion I have heard it from a Japanese person, not a Brit—unless you include the time a friend asked me if I had heard the "loony Japanese theory" that we are alike.

Indeed, the first time I heard it, I had to confirm what I was being told. It was kindly explained to me that we were both islands. That we were both constitutional monarchies. That our cultures both value politeness. It was hinted—or perhaps I inferred wrongly—that we were both a cut above our continental neighbours.

I didn't know where to begin with such an argument. England, of course, is not an island nation. The United Kingdom is, in fact made up of four distinct countries: England, Wales, Scotland and Northern Ireland. Confusing, I know, but never call a Scot "English". Japan is an archipelago. We have a queen, you have an emperor.

Perhaps the one thing more surprising than being told we are like the Japanese is hearing the English called "gentlemen". It pains me to report that nothing is further from the truth. You can meet well-mannered people in England, just as you can in any country. But I doubt there are many countries where people are so routinely uncouth. Across much of Europe, people still associate the word "English" with the word "hooligan". On holiday, we binge drink. At home, we fight over whose taxi it is. And we curse during casual conversation. I do not exempt myself from this. Most Japanese know the word "fuck" to be a terrible swear word. And it is. Except that many English use it quite casually as an intensifier. We can be describing how nice something is, and declare it "fucking beautiful". You wouldn't imagine what kind of words we use when it starts raining during a picnic. When English people visit Japan, we think we have landed in a country of good manners—rather than left one.

But these technical points and misunderstandings don't get anywhere near the main point. Which is that the English, almost to a man, will insist Japanese society is entirely and completely unlike ours.

To pick a few points at random: Japanese trains work, ours don't. England, especially London, is a multi-racial society where people look different to one another, eat different foods, worship different gods and speak differently. Tokyo is as mono-racial as any capital on earth. The English are obsessive about home ownership. Millions of young Japanese are happy to rent. Japan has earthquakes, volcanoes, typhoons, snakes, rainy seasons, terribly hot summers and (in some regions) metres of snow. We don't.

Then there are the tiny little differences in their thousands. In Japan, pedestrians have to wait twice as long for the lights to change at a crossing. On Japanese television the advertisements come on at twice the volume of the programme I was watching. That isn't allowed in England. Then they show the same nine-second advertisement twice in a row. Is it beyond them to make an 18-second advert? And couldn't they command my attention by making an interesting advertisement rather than shouting at me?

One visiting American journalist called Japan the "outnation", a kind of inversion of the word *gaikoku*. His theory was that it is Japan that is the odd one out among advanced nations. Japan's historical experience of isolation seems to have led it to operate on parallel tracks to the rest of the world. Perhaps it's trivial, but visitors wonder why their cash cards and their mobile phones work in almost every country except Japan. Sorry, but there's just no way an Englishman will come here and think: "Wow. It's really reminiscent of home." Including me.

And yet, I wonder. It's partly that I have found increasingly that people, wherever they are from, share certain values. Forgive me for making this obvious point, but it wasn't always obvious to me. When surface differences are strong, you wonder what's underneath. As a reporter, I deliberately seek out the strange and unusual in Japan. But after talking to people I almost always find there is a rational explanation for unusual customs or trends. The *freeters* may look like shirkers, but when I look at the work culture of Japanese salarymen I instinctively sympathize. I sometimes wonder how salarymen accept their hard lives, then I reflect on the poverty in Japan two generations ago and see why they might be grateful for their jobs. I have met the inventor of the *kami robo*, which are little paper figurines that can be manipulated to "wrestle". The inventor began this as a hobby but, on the advice of a friend, the *kami robo* were turned into a line of merchandise. Far from being a withdrawn *otaku* (a mysterious kind of Japanese nerd), he was as pleasant and sociable as anyone I have ever met.

And then I think of the successful examples of Anglo-Japanese cultural exchange. Looking back in history, I see a succession of great Japanese who studied in England. Hirobumi Ito, the statesman and moderniser, for example. Or the young Heihachiro Togo, who spent seven years learning seamanship with the English. Decades later he returned to England to attend the coronation of George V, and presented his old school with the flag that had flown upon his battleship Mikasa (built in England, incidentally) at the Battle of Tsushima. A hundred years later, that flag has been returned to Japan on a permanent loan to the Togo Shrine in Tokyo.

Perhaps it was in this period that Japan first conceived of itself as England's "Asian sister". The 1902 Anglo-Japanese Alliance marked not just Japan's arrival on the world stage but Britain's emergence from "splendid isolation".

In more recent years, Junichiro Koizumi studied in London, while Crown Prince Naruhito and his wife were both at Oxford. It may seem that this is one-way traffic; no Briton of great distinction has been educated in Japan.

Yet I look back at figures such as W.K. Burton, the Scot who worked here in the Meiji period and who designed the sewage systems for many Japanese cities. Mr Burton not only worked hard, he was a passionate Japanophile. Pictures show him dressed in kimono, posing Japanese-style with a fan. He himself was a keen photographer, producing the earliest collection of sumo wrestler pictures. He published pictures of the destruction caused by the earthquake of 1891 as well as pictures of the volcanoes of Japan. On the occasion of his wedding (to a Japanese lady), he produced a collection of fascinating pictures of ordinary life in Japan. Tragically, he died aged just 43 and is buried in Aoyama Cemetery.

Few Japanese have ever heard the story of how their national anthem was born. But its "midwife" was a British military bandmaster, John William Fenton, who was stationed in Yokohama. While there, Fenton was approached to teach band music to cadets from Satsuma. History tells us he stressed to them the importance of a national anthem, volunteering to compose the music if someone were to select a poem. Possibly this explains why the poem *Kimi ga Yo* was chosen, with its similarities in sentiment to *God Save the Queen*. In the end, Fenton's composition was replaced without ever being officially adopted, though we know it was performed before the Meiji Emperor in 1870.

What remains is the story of a humble British soldier taking on a group of completely unschooled musicians and helping create Japan's first military band. At the start, the band did not even have brass instruments, practicing instead on ceramic horns. Today, there are more than a half-million Japanese registered with professional, amateur and school bands.

When I think of these historical ties, I sense that

they point to some underlying connection. The former English footballer and manager Steve Perryman, who coached Shimizu S-Pulse and Kashiwa Reysol, speaks with gratitude about the enthusiasm of the Japanese players and fans. The cult British writer David Peace lived in Tokyo for 15 years, calling it "home" even as he wrote novels about life in England. Another star British writer, David Mitchell, lived for eight years in Hiroshima, an experience that has clearly influenced his writing.

It is not a rare coincidence that both Peace and Mitchell are married to Japanese. On the personal level, Japanese seem to get along with English. This was amply demonstrated during the 2002 World Cup, when many English fans were flattered to find that they were popular in Japan. I remember watching three drunken English fans flouncing into Osaka stadium singing "*ari, arigato*" to the tune of *The Great Escape*. Many of the English who made it to the tournament in Japan remember celebrating with local people in Sapporo, after England defeated Argentina, as the highlight of the trip.

Over my years in Japan, I have watched England become more Japanese. I don't just mean more sushi. When I came to Japan, I was amazed at the amount of television devoted to food and cooking. I found people's appetite for talking about food rather tiresome. "Eat to live, don't live to eat" was an old English saying. Yet today, the English are as food obsessed as any other nation on earth. Celebrity chefs, such as Jamie Oliver, are major icons. Some rate London as the best city in the world for top restaurants (albeit at high prices).

I used to puzzle at the Japanese obsession with brand name goods. I couldn't understand why people would devote a day to shopping. I tried in vain to explain that having a Louis Vuitton bag wouldn't make you a better or more interesting person, whereas reading, say, Hermann Hesse might. No one ever seemed to take my point. Now I find my countrymen just as mad about acquiring things.

Then it dawned on me. England today, after ten years of economic growth, has just caught up with the Japanese of twelve years ago. We weren't that different. We just had less money.

I used to bemoan the quality of Japanese television programmes, in which, for example, cameras would eavesdrop on single people who had been sent on a free holiday. Or some would-be celebrity is locked in a room naked and made to enter competitions to win the stuff he needs to live. "This is just a ruse to avoid having to pay for scriptwriters and actors," I fumed. "Where are the hard-hitting documentaries by investigative journalists? The British viewing public would never stand for this rubbish," I used to declare.

Today, of course, the British viewing public lap up just these kinds of programmes. We refer to it as "reality TV". In *Big Brother*, for example, people are locked in a camera-equipped house and left to bitch about each other, scheme and couple. Then there is *Celebrity Survivor*, in which has-beens and wannabes are made to eat insects for the amusement of viewers.

It seems English programming was more intellectual only until someone realized that you can amuse a lot more people for a lot less money. The English just spotted it later than the Japanese.

In the end, I cannot agree that the Japanese and the English are alike. It's just too much of a jump. (Like the time I tried to explain to my school friend that he resembled my pet cat.) But I can't dismiss the notion that there is some kind of link, too tenuous to put my finger on. Perhaps I may plunder the works of the great British comic writer Douglas Adams to find the right expression? I paraphrase: the Japanese are almost, but not quite, entirely unlike the English.

13
Temperate Island Gifts

You have to live the rest of your life by yourself on an uninhabited island. What eight pieces of music do you bring, and why?

This is the premise of a hugely successful, long-running UK radio show called *Desert Island Discs*. The guest is a celebrity or public figure who is invited to explain each choice: why this song always makes him feel better when sad, or how that song reminds him of the day he fell in love.

I think of *Desert Island Discs* every time I go to the UK on holiday. I am not restricted to eight items nor am I leaving forever. But I only have a 20 kg luggage allowance and I strive to get as much value and variety as possible from it. It will be a mix of presents and things I want for myself, a blend of luxuries and basics. I seek to cram into one suitcase a treasure trove that displays the inventiveness, deliciousness and style of Japan.

A few basic criteria apply. It makes no sense to bring anything that can be bought in England. Once, this was not a big consideration. But increasingly

Japanese products of all types can be found in the unlikeliest places. I used to bring business card holders from Mujirushi back to friends, a design classic in my view. Then it emerged that they were a popular product at Muji's London store, though some British men used them as condom holders.

Anything heavy is usually ruled out. I'd love to bring a massage chair but have yet to find one that fits in my suitcase.

Occasionally something small and dense finds its way into my suitcase, such as *miso*. When you have to lug something through airports and across cities, your sense of "cost" changes. It doesn't make sense to go to all that effort for something cheap, so I usually reach automatically for the highest quality version I can find. Of course, no one in England is going to make *miso* soup. I show them instead how to cut cucumbers and dip them into the *miso*—one of the healthiest, cheapest and most delicious snack foods ever invented.

Perishable items are no good. That rules out *edamame*, otherwise a strong candidate for inclusion. Most foreigners who try them are instant converts. I used to worry about how I would miss them when I eventually return to England. But I hear now that it is possible to buy them in London now, and they are

13 Temperate Island Gifts

even known by their Japanese name.

Japanese have an undoubted talent for snacks to accompany beer. I think I have never traveled to the UK without a packet or two of *ika* (chewy squid). It is the ideal product for the journey in terms of weight-performance. Just a few hundred grams can give a roomful of people several minutes of chewing pleasure. It is not only unavailable in the UK, the concept is new to people. People marvel at this exotic Japanese creation. And there is a great party trick you can do: my family still laughs about the time I gave some to the cat and she began to purr heavily in an almost drunken manner and tried to stuff her head into the small packet of *ika* to get more.

You might think *senbei* rice cakes and green tea, so light and so very Japanese, would be good to bring overseas. In my experience, most British people try them once and never bother again. It isn't that they don't like them. I think it's just that these fall into a straight fight with English tea and biscuits, something so dear to us and deep in our cultural psyche that we chose it ten times out of ten over the Japanese alternatives.

Mugi cha (barley tea), on the other hand, works because it can be marketed as something quite different from regular tea—a cold drink suited to summer. In the same manner, *genmaicha*—that soupy rice-based tea—works as a warming winter drink.

I wonder if some people are put off Japanese tea by the image of the tea ceremony—one of those cultural creations that people have heard of but consider awfully esoteric and ritualistic. Perhaps people imagine drinking green tea to be something like listening to atonal music—marvelous if you are educated enough to understand it, but unpleasant and complex if not.

Many of my friends in England are either Japanese or have lived in Japan at some stage. For them, the perfect gift is the little "just-add-hot-water" sachets of *ochazuke* or bottles of *furikake* flakes—both of which can turn a simple bowl of rice into a meal. So much flavour, so much of Japan, in something so light.

Even people who have never been to Japan are astounded by the transformative power of some of its products. *Goma* (sesame) dressing and *wafu* ("Japanese") dressing enjoy a very high approval rating for their ability to transform a few leaves of lettuce and a tomato into a treat. Japanese bath salts, too, seem to be more luxurious than (cheaper) English ones. Perhaps because the same water is used for up to ten baths in Japan, bath salts can easily be five times as

13 Temperate Island Gifts

expensive without putting people off?

I like to throw into the mix something that shows the odd inventiveness of Japanese gadgetry. Usually it is something I have reported on for a story. The next time I go home I know it will be the Nap Vieeb, a tiny piece of plastic you attach to your ear and which buzzes you awake the moment you nod off at the wheel or at work. My father stands to inherit an air-conditioned shirt, which blows air around your body as you work on a hot day. People are never sure whether they are more impressed or amused. Usually it is a mixture of both. "Only in Japan," they say.

In the cooler months, *kairo* are an automatic choice. England is cold, but no one ever came up with the idea of creating little portable bags of warmth. I think how different my memories of schooldays might have been had I had a little heat source in my pockets as I waited for the bus in the rain.

In summer, I bring *tatami* slippers. Light, cheap, comfortable and attractive. An ideal combination. I have also brought *yukata*, which people use as dressing gowns. People love the gorgeous designs and the glorious fabric, but the day is not yet here when they will wear them outside the house. The attention would be just too much.

For years, Japanese pottery has been a staple; little *o-chokko* sake cups in particular because so much design is fitted into something so small. Japanese paper fans are among the most practical and elegant inventions ever. Chopsticks, too, I used to bring until I one day realised my parents now had a drawer full of lovely but unused 100 yen chopsticks brought to them over the years.

One day recently I discovered a rich new category for presents when a friend told me that Japanese lead the world in luxury kitchen knives. Of course—all that sushi slicing! Another revelation, after more than a decade in Tokyo, is that you can buy little cast-off pieces of kimono silk and *chirimen* for 100 and 200 yen to use for wrapping presents. It's a cheap and effective way to enhance the pleasure of a simple gift. I never pass the Bakuro Yokoyama district without stopping by a certain shop to buy one of two little pieces of cloth.

Eventually, perhaps years from now, I will compile a tape of my favourite Japanese pieces of music. But I am sorry to say that it will probably be only one 90 minute tape. And it isn't something I expect to be handing out to lots of friends. I come across a Japanese song I really like about once every two years. Then

13 Temperate Island Gifts

there are the ones that you include not so much on merit as because they remind you of a time and place.

In tribute to *Desert Island Discs*, the eight songs that are certain to make it onto my tape are: 1) that song they always play at Okinawan restaurants, 2) *Haru Yo, Koi*, which has a rare, haunting quality, 3) *Aka Tombo*, perhaps the only Japanese traditional song I liked the first time I heard it, 4) the theme tune from *Project X*, since just about everyone in Japan seems to have bought it, 5) *Ue o Muite Arukō*, since everybody in the world seems to have bought it, 6) Kome Kome Club's *Kimi Ga Iru Dake De*, the first "omnipresent" song of my time in Japan, 7) the Hanshin Tigers' song, a rousing number from a rowdy crowd and 8) the song from *Spirited Away*, which reminds me of a lazy summer, when my newspaper was so full of the Iraq War that your poor Tokyo correspondent only got to write two or three stories, including one about this fascinating film about a girl trapped in a world of monsters.

Perhaps the heaviest item I will bring is Japanese beer. I admit it makes little sense to carry beer to England, a country with such a rich array of beers. But people always like to try something new and I like to show them that the Japanese are talented brewers—it's something few expect. I used to bring sake and *shōchū*, but no one seemed to "get it". But the beers have been a success. People like the designs of the cans as much as the rich flavours of such beers as Ginga Kogen and Yona Yona Ale.

By now, I am probably running low on suitcase space. But I can still squeeze in a few pieces of paper. Some decades ago it seems the *Yomiuri* newspaper give away reprints of Ando Hiroshige's *100 Famous Views of Edo* to its subscribers. Today, one can find these prints on sale on internet auctions and flea markets for as little as 200 yen. The view of the fireworks at Ryogoku, or the irises at Horikiri, or the hawk soaring above Fukagawa, or indeed almost any of the prints make wonderful gifts that are received with a gratitude that makes you feel embarrassed to have paid so little.

And so to England to share out the joys of Japan. And then to the next question. I can bring back 20 kg of luggage from England. What do I bring?

14
Confessions of a Tokyo Correspondent

Mea culpa. If you have ever been overseas and been surprised by the obscure and sometimes embarrassing things that foreigners know about Japan, I have to admit it's my fault. Or at least partly.

Here are some of the things I knew from newspapers before I came to Japan. Japanese people go to bars not only to drink, but to sample pure oxygen and varieties of purest air bottled at various mountain locations. A melon costs 50 pounds. It is possible to buy used knickers from vending machines.

All of this I considered nonsense. Not necessarily untrue, but hardly important. I resolved that when I became a journalist I would not pursue such trivia, but would write real stories of great importance to help British people understand Japan better. I would never condescend to write irrelevant stories for the amusement of the readership.

Of course, I failed. I have propagated as many daft stories as any other reporter in Tokyo. I have seen my name on stories that I wished I could scrub from the record, and that I would hate to show to Japanese people. Please let me try to explain how it happens.

One problem is the low level of "Japan literacy" among British readers. Almost none of them have been to Japan. Few have read books about Japanese society, seen Japanese films, or have even met Japanese people socially. This means people don't have the ability to spot when the story is off-centre, or even wrong.

Tokyo correspondents find themselves in the odd position of being the primary explainers of Japan to large numbers of our countrymen. It's a responsibility I don't really embrace. I am far from perfect. But the bigger problem is the way newspapers such as *The Daily Telegraph* work.

Usually, a Tokyo correspondent is not important within the newspaper. Newspapers spend their budgets on star sportswriters, entertaining columnists and analysts of domestic politics. Home news reporters are at least based in the office, where they may exert some influence, whereas a Tokyo correspondent is physically remote. The limited space in the newspaper is allotted largely to the "big beasts". And we don't have the clout to insist our copy goes in unchanged.

It may be difficult to believe, but I was hired by the

foreign editor of *The Daily Telegraph*, the best-selling quality daily paper in Britain, without ever having met him. I had sent my CV, written a few stories on a trial basis and talked on the phone. But it was a year before I met the people who ordered (and cut and killed) my stories. Before then, I was just a voice on the end of the phone. In over six years at the *Telegraph* I have not met or talked to any of the three men who have been editor in chief. It's a sorry indication of how important Japan is to them.

Foreign news coverage is overwhelmingly dominated by the US and the main countries of Europe. The Middle East is covered as an ongoing story. China, perhaps even India, outranks Japan. The *Telegraph* carries more Australian news than Japanese (the readers are more interested in what other English-speakers are up to, it seems). I pity my poor colleagues in South America, who have even more of a struggle.

Of course, a newspaper also has to reflect news value. And, most of the time, Japan seems to have little direct impact on British readers. Japanese registered most strongly on the British consciousness in the 1980s, when Japan was perceived (wrongly) as an economic threat. In the years since, news organizations have progressively downgraded their presence in Japan.

So many of the things that correspondents rely on for news stories just don't seem to happen in Japan. One party does not dramatically seize power from another ("LDP stays in power, loses 14 seats" is not much of a story). We get no anger on the streets. No riots or mass demonstrations. Thankfully, no war. Japanese politicians are poor communicators: they don't make moving speeches or provide many illuminating quotes.

We have to seize on personality: the "cold pizza" Obuchi, "gaffe-prone" Mori, and "eccentric" Koizumi with his wild hair and Elvis fixation. At election times, and when leaders change, we have tried to put out prominent stories. But maintaining a flow of stories—a "narrative"—is nearly impossible. I estimate that fewer than one in ten *Telegraph* readers can remember Mr Koizumi's name. And fewer than one in a hundred will remember his predecessor.

Sometimes we have tried to explain Koizumi's "bold" policies, but Post Office privatization is hardly an issue that sets the world ablaze. Even when change does come, it seems to happen at glacial pace. When a bill is being talked about and prepared for two years, on what individual day is it news?

As Japan's economy soared to giddy heights, people took interest in Japan. If it had collapsed in chaos it would have been news too. But it has fallen in slow motion. Unemployment crept up. Social chaos did not ensue. The government was not turfed out. When to seize on this subject matter? We have covered the emergence of "*freeters*", the growing problem of homelessness, the rising suicide rate among middle-aged men . . . But mostly they were short stories at intervals of several months.

During my time as a Tokyo correspondent, only once, in 2001, did foreign media suddenly become interested in Japan's economy, after finance minister Kiichi Miyazawa remarked that Japan's finances were "on the point of collapse". It caused little fuss in Japan. The situation had not changed from a week before. People had not come to a sudden realization. Nor did it signal a huge immediate shift in policy. It's just that one newspaper jumped on the "collapse" comment and a frenzy followed. Then, a week later, everyone forgot about it.

Which leaves Japan as what we call a "colour" story. Or, a source of "whacky" stories if you prefer. This is a rich vein, our bread and butter even. Take robots, for example. It's not that Japan is the only country in the world that makes robots. It's the way Japan makes ones that look funny: robots that look like humans, that play trumpets, that swim like and resemble fish . . . When you have two pages of death and destruction in Iraq, what better for the next page than a picture of a glowing robot conducting an orchestra?

Sometimes, Japan seems to have evolved in isolation from the rest of the world. The way kids dress in Harajuku raises eyebrows. Most correspondents have written about the *para para* dance, *loose socks* or *atsuzoko* platform boots when they were in fashion. Who can forget *tamagotchi*?

People love stories that Japan is changing, that its youth are different from its elders—the stereotypical serious, grey-suited salaryman and submissive housewife. Perhaps that is why, every now and again, some editor in London orders a piece on how Japanese women are becoming more assertive and "breaking free". Usually the paper flies in a woman reporter for this task, who then totally fails to understand what is going on and finds everything she sees a vindication of the starting assumption.

Not so long ago, a *Sunday Times* reporter concluded that Princess Sayako's marriage showed how Japanese women were standing up for themselves. How? She thought the princess had, for the love of commoner, defied tradition by upping sticks and walking out on the imperial family and a life of luxury.

"Sayako, who works as an ornithologist, will live in her own flat, make her own *bentō* boxes, learn to drive, and is even said to enjoy a tipple. This is pretty unprecedented behaviour," the confused visitor reported.

Another favourite anecdote among correspondents is the economics writer whose story was based around a key metaphor: that the hidden dangers in Japan's economy were like the invisible pollution that causes Japanese to wear face masks. It's an interesting way of putting it, but somehow his imagery is less striking if you know that the face masks are to stop pollen from cedar trees.

Profound change is occurring in Japan, but of a kind ill-suited for daily newspapers because they prize news. Japan's collapsing birth rate is effectively a population implosion. But how to tell the story?

Once, I remember illustrating this demographic change by writing about the release of the Primopuel, a childlike doll. The doll was aimed at young women, who are increasingly without children, but proved an unexpected hit with older women, who regret their lack of grandchildren. It may seem an odd way into the subject, but without some such angle a newspaper is unlikely to run a story on such a dry topic. A quirky "peg" and colourful picture engage readers.

At one time I wrote a list of key words to remind me what Japan stories my editors like. I threw it away because I no longer need a bit of paper to remind me: World War II, sumo, yakuza, geisha, imperial family, women, youth trends, Article Nine, odd crimes. Under that, I might have added a range of subjects that can work if a suitably interesting development happens (pachinko, Takarazuka, kimono, *enka*...)

By any yardstick, some of the crimes that occur in Japan are remarkable. I think of all those people paying cash to the Ho-no-Hana "foot cult". Or the fake "Prince Arisugawa" inviting guests to his "royal wedding". Or the "harem" in Tokyo, where the man was divorcing one wife and marrying the next the same day. I make no excuses for recounting these stories in the paper. Japanese lap them up just as much as overseas readers. I just wish there were more serious Japan stories in our pages for balance.

Many correspondents find their newspaper is like a machine over which they have little leverage. With relatively minor editing, a sensitively written story intended to reveal something about Japanese society can be turned into an embarrassing article that just pokes fun. For example, I have tried to talk about Japan's ageing society and how Japan is seeking solutions with technology. To lighten the story, I suggested we use as an example a "robot seal" pet, developed for use in care homes for the elderly. Petting the seal is believed to have healing qualities, and help with the feelings of isolation many elderly people suffer in environments where they can't keep real pets.

For two days my office bombarded me with appeals to rewrite. "It cries out for a lighter touch," they said. In the end they rewrote it themselves so that it said nothing, or almost nothing, about Japan's ageing society. It became a story about whacky elderly Japanese playing with robot toys.

This kind of rewriting is routine, but none the less sickening for it. The process works as follows. First, the writer is pressed into cooperating as far as possible. He will be asked to send more information on the weird aspect of the story, even if he is not keen to stress that. He is promised space for the story, "if only we can fix" this or that aspect. However, the extra words will inevitably be used not *in addition to* serious copy, but to replace it.

Secondly, the story's top line will be changed. The emphasis will change from "Japan trying to cope with its aging society" to "Robot seals pushed into action" or some such. The headline, which correspondents have no control over, will be similarly daft. This "tweaking" changes the whole impression of the story.

The paragraph order will be changed. The first four or five paragraphs will be used not to develop the anecdote about robot seals into a wider story about society, but to ham up the weirdness of it all.

At the bottom of the copy, often literally a single line, will be a reference to the issue at hand. For example, "Japan is seeking ways to deal with its aging society." Readers will not come away with any deeper understanding of the issues. Indeed, as editors know, most readers never reach that final line. It seems to be there so that editors can tell correspondents that some part of the analysis was kept, but that the rest was regrettably "squeezed for space reasons".

My personal view is that whacky anecdotes are fair if they are true and tell us something about society, not just played for cheap laughs. The published story should be something that the writer is happy to show—and justify—to the people who appear in it.

Sadly, that is often not the case.

I can remember a story about how Japanese attitudes to pets were changing. As an example I cited apartment blocks specifically designed for people with pets. I intended a story about how Tokyo is turning pet-friendly. My editors changed it to a story about how the "Japanese obsession with cleanliness" has led construction firms to put "dog showers" at the entrance to apartment buildings. I was too embarrassed to send a copy of the story to those I interviewed and quoted within.

On occasion, papers deliberately falsify. Once I was commissioned to write about Kobe Beef, after an editor in London read that the cows are fed on beer and massaged regularly. When I went to Kobe I found this to be untrue at the particular farm that I visited—and grossly exaggerated in general. I wrote up what I saw. But time and money had been spent on the story and space had been allotted. The editor was waiting for his story of cows living a life of luxury more wonderful than many humans. And so my reporting was completely rewritten in London. When I saw the newspaper, I was unsure whether to laugh or cry. The opening "onscene" description was littered with factual mistakes, including reference to "gallons of premium lager". An English teacher friend has often pressed me to give him my original version and the published copy to use in class as a literary "spot the difference" test for students. Even the photograph was from a farm in a totally different part of Japan.

Perhaps it doesn't matter if a British newspaper perpetuates a myth about beer-guzzling cows. But sloppiness occurs regularly and can happen in more serious stories. On the day of his election to prime minister, Mr Koizumi said he was in favour of amending Japan's "pacifist constitution". *The Daily Telegraph* managed to headline this: "New leader in Japan wants right to wage war", which is dangerously misleading.

In 2005, I wrote about Japan's controversial "nationalist" school textbooks that had angered Chinese. The editing swept aside all subtleties. No reader would know that there was a wide range of textbooks available, or that the single most controversial history book had so far been adopted by fewer than 1 percent of all schools in Japan.

On that occasion I emailed a letter of complaint to my desk, which they ignored. Then, after a few too many beers, I sent a similar note to the letters page of the paper pointing out the ludicrous lack of context in that story by Colin Joyce in Tokyo. I promptly forgot about it until they contacted me to say they wanted to publish the letter, apparently not having noticed that my name was the same as the author of the piece.

So why continue? Because there are times when it goes fantastically. I remember being given generous space in the paper when the sumo wrestlers of the Isenoumi Stable started crime patrols. A million readers would have seen a long story about the concern over rising crime in a once famously safe society. I had the honour to write an obituary for the historian Saburo Ienaga, one of the people I most admired. I have met and talked to hundreds of extraordinary and fascinating people. Sometimes, I can get that excitement across, introduce to readers something they never knew about or would normally not care about. I think of the time I wrote about the discovery in England—and return to Japan—of Togo's battle flag from the 1905 Battle of Tsushima, at a time when the Japanese press barely covered the anniversary of this famous battle.

There is much to admire in Japanese newspapers, such as their essential reliability and the work ethic of their extensive networks of reporters. Even more, I admire the readers. It is a testament to their literacy and public-mindedness that in a country of 127 million, over 24 million broadsheets are sold every day. Britain's four quality dailies (*Telegraph*, *Times*, *Guardian* and *Independent*) sell a little over 2 million copies, in a country with a population roughly half that of Japan.

But perhaps Japan could learn from Britain. The *Telegraph* at least is trying to cover foreign news, even if the results are often unsatisfactory. Japanese papers, despite their huge budgets, devote very little space to international events. When I show Japanese people copies of the *Telegraph* they are fascinated by the range of stories, the mix of serious and light pieces, features and sports. The writing style is varied, the pictures and design are carefully considered. (They also note how many stories are by, for and about women.)

I make to myself the excuse that if I left it would not be any better. Indeed, my replacement would probably have to start at the beginning fighting the same battles again that I have tried to fight. But there's no point in denying it. With infuriating regularity I and my counterparts in Japan are writing about things trivial or daft, and missing the big issues of the day. Like I said, it's my fault, and for that I am sorry.

15
Gaijin Dilemmas

I am having lunch at the *Newsweek* canteen in New York seated beside a British art director and an Indian editorial assistant. I tell them that I am visiting from Japan and they say in unison: "What's it like being a *gaijin*?"

For a moment I am too surprised to answer: how the hell did they know the "G word"? Perhaps it was from the James Clavell novel of that title. Perhaps it was the cartoon strip by the American Tim Ernst, which portrayed some of the struggles of the foreigner in Japan. Or perhaps the word has seeped into the English language—along with awareness that somehow the experience of the Westerner in Tokyo is particularly odd.

Perhaps I should have regaled them with anecdotes of hitting my head on doorframes and of being made to sing *God Save the Queen* without backing music at karaoke. But I cannot help feeling that for the long-term Japan resident the question is actually a bit more serious than that. How do you live and work in a society where you are always an outsider?

To some extent living in a foreign culture is an assault on your personality and your learned behaviour. One response is to go native, but this is something like a religious conversion, a leap of faith based on the assumption that you can find happiness by changing yourself and giving in to something bigger than you. It almost always ends in tears. At the other extreme is the "no surrender" approach, when people insist on the primacy of their own culture. Such obduracy is of course repugnant and leads to a kind of isolation.

Inevitably, the answer lies somewhere in between—creating a host of little dilemmas to be resolved as they occur, requiring complex calculations and careful weighing of the pros and cons. Sometimes they are important decisions. Such as what to do when your ingrained sense of fairness clashes with a Japanese sense of *giri* (obligation). Sometimes it is a trivial decision. Do you say "*moshi moshi*" or "hello" when you answer the phone, if half your calls are from English people and half from Japanese?

I won't try to answer for you. Not least because I know I get it wrong embarrassingly often. I have offended Japanese friends while trying to treat them as I would friends from home. I have argued a point of

15 Gaijin Dilemmas

principle at length, then arrived home to realize it wasn't worth the trouble; all I have done is work myself up and make someone dislike me. But perhaps I can give you a sense of what it feels like to be a *gaijin*.

You are hot and irritated and trying to get somewhere. A Japanese man with a "light saber" is telling you not to cross the road against the red light. But there are no cars coming. You know Japanese people would wait patiently and you know the man would be distraught if you ignore his efforts. Do you cross?

Your Japanese colleagues all work late every day. But you have finished your work by five pm. In your culture—and your contract—that means you can go home. Do you leave at five? Do you hang around for a bit longer? Or do you volunteer to help a colleague?

In the office there are two or three Japanese people who resent you because you have less work than the local staff. Do you try to win them round, or is it their problem?

A Japanese high school teacher tells you he is marrying a former pupil. Do you congratulate him? Or do you find it creepy?

A Japanese friend who used to live in England invites you round to his house. Do you need to bring a present?

Since this is Japan you take your shoes off in your house. But you can never feel as obsessive about it as Japanese do. Your friend comes from England and doesn't want to do it. Do you make him?

Do you say "*kampai*" or "cheers"? (Does it smack of "going native" to say "*kampai*" when with other *gaijin*? Have you ever seen a mixed group of Japanese saying "cheers" and English saying "*kampai*"?)

You have spent years learning the lingo and ask a man in perfectly clear Japanese if he knows a pharmacy nearby. He replies "no" in accented English and makes a big X with his arms in front of you. How do you react? How do you react if you are, say, German, and English isn't even your native language? The man probably doesn't realize he is being rude—do you tell him?

A well-intentioned man tells you that "you are a good *gaijin*". Do you accept that as a compliment? Or do you sense that if you did something not to his liking he would label you a "*furyō gaijin*" ("a bad foreigner")?

Do you mind the word "*gaijin*"? Or do you prefer "*gaikokujin*"? Is there a difference?

The newspaper reports that crimes by foreigners

are up, without pointing out that foreigners commit a tiny portion of crimes in Japan and fewer per capita than Japanese. How do you feel?

Your neighbour, whom you know to be a kindly person, mentions her worries about crimes by foreigners. You have never heard her mention her worries about crimes by yakuza—an organization of violent thugs preying on society and dealing in drugs and prostitution. What do you say?

A policeman stops you to check your bicycle and see your alien registration card. Do you let him, knowing you will be on your way in 30 seconds? Or do you ask him why he is doing so?

You are being unreasonable and you know it. You've had a bad day and are over-reacting, but you can't stop. Later you feel bad. Do you feel extra bad because Japanese who saw you will think less of British people now? Are you always an ambassador for your country?

You are walking along a nearly empty street, not far from your house, and you spot another foreigner walking towards you. Do you nod? Say hello? Ignore him and walk past? If so, where do you look if you are trying not to look at him?

Most people who live overseas find it therapeutic

to moan with a compatriot from time to time about the irritations of life in Belgium, Brazil, Britain or wherever. You are having this kind of whinge about life in Japan with a *gaijin* friend on a train. Obviously, some Japanese passengers can understand all of what you are saying. Many can get the gist of it. But no one in Japan would ever intervene and ask you to stop. Are you being bad mannered? Is it even worse because Japanese don't usually argue back at you or tell you to go back to your own country?

For the nth time someone asks you if you "can eat" *nattō*. The person asking is just curious and means no harm. What is your answer? And can you keep answering politely for another year or two years?

A Japanese friend has done something quite bad but will not defend himself. You cannot be sure if he is acknowledging guilt in some subtle Japanese way, or refusing to acknowledge your point. Perhaps he wants to say sorry but the un-Japanese aggression of your verbal assault is the problem. Or perhaps he doesn't see what he did wrong. Do you keep drilling away, or do you drop it?

You have received very bad service from a shop. You ask why it happened. They say "*mōshi wake gozaimasen*" ("there's no excuse") several times. This is

15 Gaijin Dilemmas

not an answer to your question "why". Do you accept the apology?

You come across a stupid system. For example, you have to pay a commission to withdraw your own money from your own account on a weekend. You raise the matter, but the manager is clearly only pretending to listen to you. You infer, probably correctly, that he sees you as just an annoying *gaijin*, rather than a customer raising a legitimate question. How do you react?

You are invited to a wedding by someone to whom you are not incredibly close. You know you are supposed to bring 30,000 yen cash. You cannot help feeling the Japanese system is odd—you only spent around 20,000 yen on your sister's wedding present. Do you feign a business trip? Or accept that weddings cost money? And is it insulting to your sister to spend more on someone else?

By arguing ferociously, you have gotten a reduction on an over-priced meal at a restaurant with hidden charges. Have you stood up against lousy cheats who take advantage of the fact that Japanese so rarely complain? Or have you upset the "*wa*" (harmony) of Japanese society?

You are writing for a Japanese readership. Do you

deliberately avoid mentioning anything negative about Japan? Or do you try to be honest about the good and the bad and hope they can see your point of view?

16
Smells Like Pickled Eel

***"Unagi** no tsukemono mitaina nioi da."*

For reasons I struggle to explain, this was my first full sentence of Japanese. "It smells like pickled eel."

The simple explanation is that I, and a lot of English, have a strange sense of humour. More than I wanted to dazzle people with my linguistic skills, I wanted to confuse and amuse them. So I rote learned this sentence and reeled it out whenever I passed the perfume counter in a department store or whenever I was invited to sample a new food

Then one day someone pointed out that there was no such thing as pickled eel.

Aha, but there is! It is a local dish of East London, sold alongside fish & chips and pie & mash at cafés around the region, including those near the market in my hometown, Romford.

When I tell this to Japanese people, it invites a barrage of questions: How does it taste? How it is prepared? What does it look like? And what does it smell like?

And I flounder. I am not really sure . . . You see, I

have never tried it.

Japanese, I realized, do not just eat food. They talk about it, relish it and even "visit" it. Before I came to Japan it had never occurred to me that someone could go on holiday with the specific purpose of enjoying the food. I had always seen the "eating" part of the holiday as an incidental bonus.

This cultural gap was obvious to me when I saw the silent astonishment at my admission that I have never eaten the traditional fare of my hometown. I had no idea how it was made. I knew that it is reputed to taste awful—eaten out of perverse pride rather than for pleasure. I know that the eel sits in a rather off-putting jelly, and is for that reason called jellied eels.

I came to see that it is not just that Japanese *food* is different, but the whole *culture of food*. Actually, not just different but better. Japan not only has good food, it is a nation of gourmands.

Therein, oddly, lay a glimmer of hope for me in an argument I seemed to keep losing. Japanese would tell me—sometimes rather smugly, I felt—that Japanese food was great and that English food was awful. But they are usually sufficiently interested in the subject to listen to my views on English food.

I don't agree that English food is terrible. (And I

am still unsure why the Japanese, who I know to be modest and polite, aren't at all polite or modest on this issue.)

English food is far better than many people realize. But we lack the marketing, the attention to detail and the devotion to food that one sees in Japan—things which turn a meal into an experience.

It may be odd to start a defence of English cooking by mentioning jellied eels, which, by all accounts, tastes genuinely unpleasant. But it does flag up the fact that there are lots of foods in England that foreign people have never heard of. And it is not the only example of food that people eat despite the taste: I might cite *gyūdon*, which has a similar function and fan base.

There are lots of things that taste better in England than Japan: bacon, cheese, bread and beer, for example. You can get nice bread in Japanese bakeries, but does it have to be seven variations of sugary white bread? England is blessed with far greater variety: wheatgerm, rye bread, even pumpernickel and other heavy continental breads.

The British deserve to be better known for their cheeses. There are some 700 local varieties, each with a distinct flavor. But these are rarely sold outside the

UK. In Japan, you often see Australian Cheddar. If you are ever in the UK, try the real thing—which actually comes from England's West Country, where the village of Cheddar is located. Mature cheddar is so strongly flavoured that a tiny amount grated onto a baked potato will transform it utterly. Or you could try Somerset Brie, which shows we can imitate French cheese, or Wensleydale from Yorkshire. Stilton—a rich blue cheese—is a personal favourite that I always look forward to tasting when I visit home.

Please excuse me if I launch a counter-attack. While acknowledging that Japanese food is very, very good, I would boldly argue that its key ingredient—Japanese rice—is over-rated. It's high in calories and not very versatile. It doesn't have a wide range of vitamins and nutrients, lacks roughage, and the main varieties of Japanese rice aren't very varied. It's also expensive and takes an impractical amount of time to prepare properly. From washing (couldn't one of the numerous handlers between farmer and consumer do that?) to soaking, through the cooking and waiting, it takes almost two hours. This is hardly ideal when you get home from work hungry at 9 pm. I sometimes wonder if rice isn't the real reason why Japanese housewives have to stay at home and cook, rather than

16 SMELLS LIKE PICKLED EEL

have careers.

An eccentric friend from university once tried to engage his new girlfriend in conversation with the line: "What's your favourite carbohydrate?" I believe the consensus among my friends was that, firstly, this was the worst chat-up line in history. And secondly, the correct order was bread, potatoes, rice and pasta.

My hero, the novelist and journalist George Orwell, wrote *In Defence of English Cooking* way back in 1945. I am probably plagiarizing some of his arguments here—his views so influenced mine that I no longer know where his end and mine begin. Orwell pointed out the wide range of English puddings. Eccles cakes, for example, are a perfect treat. So, incidentally, is Yorkshire pudding, which is not a pudding at all but an accompaniment to roast beef, made from batter.

The tea in England is superb. Even the cheap supermarket brands—at little more than a penny a tea bag—brew up delightfully. I have never really seen the need to pay the extra for Fortnum and Mason tea. Twinings, priced somewhere in between, is my recommendation.

Certain things have changed since Orwell's day. He pointed out that few foreigners have the chance to experience real English cooking, since it is eaten overwhelmingly in the home. There was no such thing as a restaurant serving fine English foods (café food is admittedly poor). Today, some of the finest restaurants in the world are in Britain. Some of these use local ingredients and traditional ways of cooking, but others serve continental food. In 2005, 600 food critics chose the world's best establishments for *Restaurant Magazine*. English restaurants occupied 14 of the top 50 places, including the top spot.

Japanese people may disagree with my terms here. I am here praising the "food sold in Britain", rather than British cuisine per se. I have a friend who loves eating Italian food in London; and hates it in Japan. "The cheapest pasta, simply drowned in sauce," he complains. I might add that there are better Japanese restaurants in London than there are British restaurants in Japan.

For a Japanese to walk around any Tesco superstore in England would be a humbling experience. The range, quality and value-for-money of the food available is far superior to that of Japanese stores. Many supermarkets include a butcher, fishmonger and baker. I relish visiting the deli counter. The sandwiches are of high quality. The cakes, biscuits and breakfast cereals available are phenomenal.

16 SMELLS LIKE PICKLED EEL

You could drop by every day for a week and select the produce to make seven different kinds of picnics. Staples such as bread, milk, fruit and vegetables are somewhere around a third the price of Japan. As a student, I would cook a healthy plate of mushrooms in mashed potatoes and add a dash of Worcester sauce. Approximately 50 pence for a bellyful.

I want to put on record that the English invented Worcester sauce. It's called Worcester after the town in England. The "*ūsutā sōsu*" version made in Japan is a poor imitation. The real one is a condiment to be splashed lightly on certain foods. It also enlivens a glass of tomato juice. (This is what a lot of people, none of them Japanese, drink on airplanes).

I would like to add that the sandwich was invented by an Englishman—the Earl of Sandwich, hence the name. There is even a credible argument that the British invented crème brûlée. Please reflect on the genius of English cookery next time you enjoy either.

London is also the world capital of curry. It has more curry restaurants than Delhi and Mumbai combined, and the annual curry awards are taken very seriously. A curry lover is better advised to visit England than India. Curry is, no mistake, an Indian invention, but New York claims the bagel (originally

Polish) and countries all over the world have appropriated the sandwich.

In London you can try every variety of curry, whereas in India one can generally experience only the curry of the particular region you are visiting. I might also mention that one curry dish I am sure the Japanese would love is chicken tikka masala, a mild creamy tomato curry invented in Britain for people unused to hot spices.

The English are not just imitators. In Portugal they created Port Wine, as distinct and marvelous as anything the French created with grapes. The English make the best version of gin and the Scots gave us whisky, though I personally cannot abide either drink.

It could be argued that the world's finest marmalade is made by Frank Cooper of Oxford (the city where I went to university) and the finest jams are made by Wilkin and Sons from Tiptree in Essex, which happens to be where my parents now live. They make a phenomenal range, including such rarities as Green Fig jam and Loganberry. Incidentally, Wilkin and Sons is the brand of jam that James Bond ate—a man of fine taste, even if he is fictional.

I would lastly sing the praise of porridge oats, which is the traditional breakfast of Scotland. The finest quality oats can be bought in industrial quantities with loose change. Yet it is quick to cook, warms you up on a cold day and is very healthy. Eaten with a banana and a sprinkle of brown sugar it is the most delicious breakfast ever devised.

By now, I hope that you will have at least begun to wonder whether the poor reputation of British food might be an unreasonable slur. If so, I may now proceed to point out the considerable shortcomings of the British culture of food. For one thing, there is the excessive consumption of junk food and sweets, which is causing an epidemic of child obesity. There is also an over-reliance on tinned food, especially the ubiquitous baked beans (tasteless beans swimming in artificial tomato sauce).

Britain also lacks the range of restaurants found in Japan. Eating out in English restaurants is expensive. It can sometimes be expensive and bad. And when it isn't expensive, you can be pretty sure it is bad. I wish there were something like the *izakaya*, where you may be punishing your liver but you are at least pleasing your stomach. The UK needs more of the kind of pleasant eating environments that you often find in Japan, places that encourage conversation and a sense of well-being as we eat.

The home *nabe* is a wonderful vehicle for pleasant social discourse. Rather than one person doing all the work, it is shared by all. Everyone can also share the smell and anticipation of the food as it cooks. It is difficult to summon up a cosier image for a cold winter evening. In Denmark there is a state of contentment known as *hygge*, which denotes the feeling of togetherness one experiences when everything is nice and snug. It struck me as the perfect word for the experience of preparing *nabe* with friends while seated under a *kotatsu*. (It is also evidence that boiled food can be good—incidentally deflecting one of the common criticisms of English cooking.)

The vast majority of English still lag behind the Japanese in their knowledge and appreciation of food. I have seen English people putting ketchup on carrots. In Japan, it is very rare to see food eaten the wrong way. Maybe it is the result of eating too much processed food, but I and other English sometimes lack the ability to listen to our taste buds—I used to drink the leftover "soup" from *udon*, until a Japanese friend pointed out that it was salty and unpleasant.

I need hardly tell you of the delights of Japanese food. *Unagi*—not pickled —I adore, and sushi of course. But what I love most about Japanese food is the way it tends to slow me down as I eat. I like the presentation, particularly the ceramics. I can hold and look at a piece of unglazed *bizen* pottery for several minutes. I am particularly fond of little *ochoko* sake cups. A nice *hashi-oki* (chopstick rest) is a treat—there is a whole shop devoted to them near Omotesando.

The way that, in Japan, you can use quite different types of plates and dishes at the same meal strikes me as relaxing and natural—just as I enjoy nibbling from one dish, then from another. It's very different from the formal English dinner, where courses follow in a strict order, the dining sets are of a uniform design, and there are lots of rules about which knife one uses for which food and which direction one passes the port. I remember being rather nervous at my first formal dinner at Oxford. Apparently, to drain the last drop of soup from your bowl you may tilt it away from yourself, not toward. And to spit out an olive seed you pretend to cough, holding your hand to your mouth.

Of course, Japanese food is known worldwide for being healthy. But people don't usually know that it is also sold, presented and eaten in moderate servings in Japan. This is crucial. It's surely no coincidence that some of the fattest people on earth live in Texas, where servings are huge. I suspect we overeat because part of our brain tells us that we should eat everything on our plate, even if we are full.

And so, I have a bold proposal—I could entrust this to nobody better. Could the Japanese please take up the challenge of reinventing jellied eels? Turn it into a *meibutsu*? I would want them to find new ways to cook it, while respecting its core tradition; to recreate it for the modern diner; to rebrand it and find ways to serve it so that, one day, people from Britain and Japan will catch a whiff from a restaurant as they walk past and sigh with pleasure: "Aah, smells like jellied eels."

17
Letter to an Incoming Correspondent

Dear John,

Congratulations on being appointed to succeed me as Tokyo correspondent of *The Daily Telegraph*. I am sure you will find the job fascinating.

I apologise for the ramshackle nature of this note. I know you will have read up about Japan and that you will want to find things out for yourself. So this isn't a comprehensive guide to living in Japan; just some random points, in no particular order, that I can recall and that would have been of use to me.

Buy some slip-on shoes. You have to take your shoes on and off a lot. Over the years slip-ons will save you hundreds of hours that might have been wasted struggling with laces in the narrowest and most congested part of a Japanese house, while you drop your shopping everywhere and wish you could get in out of the heat / cold.

Mind your head. It's not the doorframes that you are walking towards that you collide with. It's the one you're under when you are bending over the vacuum cleaner—don't jerk upright without thinking. Or it could be the cupboard door over the sink, which you left open while you made the tea.

If you do hit your head after a very bad day at the office, don't punch the door to vent your frustration. It is probably made of paper.

Plan your moment of entry onto a crowded train. Otherwise you get stuck under a waving *nakazuri* (hanging advertisement) or a strap, or find your head is inches below a super-powered cooler.

Don't put your bag on the floor of the train. Once the carriage fills up you will be unable to bend over to retrieve it.

You cannot see *kabuki* in Kabukicho.

A *pabbu* is not a pub.

Sake has an exquisite mild and pleasant taste.

Sake produces exquisitely painful hangovers.

The tea in coffee shops is not very good. Other than that, you should be delighted and amazed by the richness and quality of Japan's food culture.

Don't think too much about what you want to eat in the evening. Go to the supermarket forty minutes before closing and just pick from the selection of things with *hangaku* (half-price) stickers.

Learn twenty words of Japanese before you come. People will appreciate your efforts. Start with

17 LETTER TO AN INCOMING CORRESPONDENT

adjectives. Just being able to say *oishii, atsui, natsukashii, sugoi, kirei* and *omoshiroi* will enable you to cope with a lot of situations.

Japanese people will actually tell you that you are fluent. Don't believe them. They tell me I am tall, handsome, charming, amusing and interesting. In fact, I am tall.

Nevertheless, the Japanese are the most honest people in the world. Of course, in all countries people tell lies. But the Japanese are perhaps the only people who regularly and openly admit that this is happening, happily telling you about *honne* and *tatemae*. (This is the gap between what people actually think and their public facade.)

When a Japanese person loses an argument they say "*datte . . .*" ("because . . . "), but then don't explain.

Don't, in your first week here, get a little *hanko* chop made using some amusing *kanji* that sound out your name. If you must, don't get it legally registered. Afterwards you will be embarrassed that the name on your bank book is something odd, like 虎林 .

Japan has lots of rules and regulations. Some of them are silly and meaningless.

The sea may be perfectly warm and inviting in September. But the rule about not swimming after *o-bon*, in mid-August, turns out not to be one of the silly meaningless rules.

Japanese jellyfish cause poisonous blisters that last for months. These jellyfish proliferate as autumn approaches (see above rule).

Expect to be asked two questions a lot: "Can you eat *nattō*?" and "Do you like Japan?" Prepare your answers in advance. I advise you to answer "Yes" to the latter question. After that, though, you are free to complain about the difficulties you will inevitably face in Japan, safe in the knowledge that you have a sympathetic listener.

Find out your blood type, and your shoe size in centimeters.

People (well, young women) may tell you their hobby is shopping. Others (salarymen) may tell you their hobby is sleeping. Do not be alarmed. These are considered hobbies in Japan.

In England, you probably tried to own as much stuff as possible. In Japan, this urge must be tempered by rigorous reference to how much space you have in your apartment.

I am sure you have been learning *meishi* etiquette, which is very important. Although you can print your own business cards, everyone in Japan will believe

17 Letter to an Incoming Correspondent

whatever is written on your business card. Resist the temptation to give yourself the title "Lord of the known universe".

Avoid the company of any Westerners who tell you they are "searching for the real Japan".

Talk to Japanese people and listen to them. It's not just your job; you will learn a lot.

Travel. It is a diverse country. If you can't get much time off, go to Yokohama once a month, Shimoda twice a year and climb Mount Takao once a year.

Eat lunch out regularly. The food is good and, at the standard price of 1,000 yen, it is a bargain.

Try to avoid getting invited to a wedding. It is ruinously expensive and not much fun.

The weather is fundamentally different. In England, it usually rains a bit then stops, so it doesn't prevent you from doing anything. In Japan, it tips down buckets for days on end, and just walking to the end of the street you can get as wet as if you had jumped in a lake. On a hot day, sitting in the shade doesn't work either.

Eating while walking is considered bad manners. Chewing gum on a train is considered good manners. (I'm not sure why in either case).

If you ever find yourself working in a Japanese

company, you may notice that Japanese people can't leave without doing hours of overtime. You can.

Sometimes people will tell you "when in Rome do as the Romans". My slightly less pithy version, formulated for Japan, is: "When in Rome, know the Roman customs and respect them. However, if the Romans have some daft rules, you aren't forbidden to argue politely against them. But they aren't obliged to change them. Most Romans are very reasonable people and won't expect you to follow all their customs. Indeed, many Romans wish they did some things a bit differently themselves."

Lastly, I can think of no better advice than that which our illustrious countryman, the 19th century Japanologist Basil Hall Chamberlain, told Lafcadio Hearn on his arrival in Japan: "Do not fail to write down your first impressions as soon as possible. They are evanescent, you know; they will never come to you again, once they have faded out; and yet of all the strange sensations you may receive in this country you will feel none so charming as these."

Good luck.

Profile

Colin Joyce is a proud native of Romford, one of England's most unloved towns. Born in 1970, he studied Ancient and Modern History at Oxford University, where some of the tutors assumed he was stupid because of his funny accent and short temper.

His exam results amazed them and he won a scholarship to study Japanese in Kobe in 1992. There, his striking inability to learn Japanese finally proved those doubting tutors right. He stayed in Japan largely because of his stubborn refusal to leave until he could pass muster at the language. He is useless with money, but a lover of good beer and football. He believes it is no coincidence that Japan's economy got worse during his time in Japan, but that its standards of football and beer improved immeasurably. He taught for two years at a prefectural high school in Saitama before realizing he was unsuited to a job that required punctuality on a daily basis. He worked for *Newsweek Japan* for four years and still writes for the magazine, including a blog for its website. He was the Tokyo correspondent for *The Daily Telegraph*, Britain's best-selling quality daily paper, for seven years until 2007. He is currently a freelance writer, based in New York.

How to Japan
A Tokyo Correspondent's Take

2009(平成21)年8月25日　　第1刷発行
2014(平成26)年10月5日　　第8刷発行

著者　　コリン・ジョイス
　　　　©2009 Colin Joyce
発行者　溝口明秀
発行所　NHK出版
　　　　〒150-8081 東京都渋谷区宇田川町41-1
　　　　電話 0570-002-046（編集）
　　　　　　 0570-000-321（注文）
　　　　ホームページ　　http://www.nhk-book.co.jp
　　　　振替 00110-1-49701
印刷　　光邦／大熊整美堂
製本　　三森製本

定価はカバーに表示してあります。
落丁・乱丁本はお取り替えいたします。
本書の無断複写（コピー）は、著作権法上の例外を除き、
著作権侵害となります。

Printed in Japan
ISBN 978-4-14-035084-3 C0082

ブックデザイン／畑中猛